Home for the Holidays

A poetic anthology of verse celebrating the gathering of families during the fall and winter holidays.

Paul Gilliland

Editor-in-Chief

Southern
Arizona
Press

Southern Arizona Press

Southern Arizona Press

Southern
Arizona
Press

The mission of Southern Arizona Press is to promote the works of self-published and lesser-known unpublished authors and poets to the rest of the world through publishing themed and unthemed anthologies and assisting in the publication and promotion of their works.

It is our desire to make the voices of these aspiring poets and authors available to as wide an audience as possible with the belief that no writer of poetry or literature should ever have to pay to have their works published.

Home for the Holidays

If you would like your work to be considered for future anthologies, please visit us at:
http://www.southernarizonapress.com/current-submissions/
for a full list of current open anthology submissions and submission guidelines.

Published by Southern Arizona Press
Sierra Vista, Arizona 85635
www.southernarizonapress.com

Follow us on Facebook at:
https://www.facebook.com/SouthernArizonaPress

Format, cover design, and edits by Paul Gilliland, Editor-in-Chief, Southern Arizona Press

Cover Art: Image by Muhammad Ragab from Pixabay
Interior images: Image byOpenClipart-Vectors from Pixabay
Free for use under the Pixabay Content License

Poets photos Copyright © retained by submitting poets

ISBN: 9781960038494

TABLE OF CONTENTS

Pat Severin, a retired teacher and member of SCBWI, has been writing poetry for many years. Her poems are regularly featured in the online magazines, *The Agape Review*, *The Clay Jar Review*, *Pure in Heart Stories*, *Heart of Flesh Literary Journal*, and *The Way Back to Ourselves*. She is honored to have contributed to the Southern Arizona Press Anthologies. This is her tenth anthology.

She is also a published contributor to the books, *I Chose You, Rescue Dogs and their Humans*, *Chicken Soup for the Soul: Lessons Learned From My Dog*, and the upcoming book, *When Love Wags a Tail*, out next year.

Her personal ministry is sending weekly cards of encouragement to those going through difficult times.

THE TRUE JOY OF CHRISTMAS

When winter is approaching, we expect the cold it brings,
The freezing ice, the drifting snow, the search for warmer things.
The chill begins with Halloween, Thanksgiving on its heels,
The cold sets in as Christmas nears, much busier it feels…

Because we've got to buy the gifts, perhaps there's travel plans,
Check out the lights, go get the tree, and put it in the stand,
Send out the cards, wrap presents, too, and then to decorate.
There must be something else to do…what do we celebrate?

There is another reason for this festive time of the year
That's spent with loved ones gathered close…but is it really clear
That Christ, God's Son was born that day so many years ago?
Could it be overshadowed by the things that often go…

Before the greatest gift of all, that Babe who brought salvation,
Who offers all eternal life, who prompts this celebration?
God's promise kept, His only Son, should never be forgotten
Because He came for everyone, the wealthy to down-trodden.

So, as you plan your holiday and those you love are near,
Remember why we celebrate this season every year.
We wish for you this Christmastime the blessings that it brings
And may you know God's love for you, from there our true joy
    springs.

WHAT'S THE HURRY?

Say, what's the hurry, it's too soon.
It's barely Halloween!
The stores decked out with Christmas fare
With trees and grass still green?

So, c'mon can't we take our time,
Enjoy these days of fall,
Watch winter slowly usher in
Our senses to enthrall,

Anticipate the time when we
As family come together,
And take the opportunity
To snuggle in cold weather,

To bundle up in comfy clothes,
All cozy by the fire.
The sipping of hot chocolate is
What freezing hands desire.

Then as the day comes closer still
For thankfulness and praise,
Share blessings, often undeserved,
Not on just one, but days,

To contemplate Thanksgiving Day
And what it really means.
It's much more than too much to eat
And tighter fitting jeans.

It's rather taking stock of all
The Good Lord gives each day,
For whether much or just enough
Our thankful hearts repay...

By giving back, by sharing, too,
And in so doing, lives...
A life that's full of untold wealth
That freely loves, forgives.

And from this holiday begins
Our memories of Christ's birth,
A birth much more significant
Than any here on earth.

So often Christmas time is marred
By selfishness and having,
When value's measured by the price,
And bargains by the grabbing.

Why can't our Christmas truly be
A birthday for our Savior,
Who came to give eternal life,
God's Son born in a manger.

When it's your birthday you get gifts,
Why can't we do the same
By giving presents to the poor,
Gifts given in His name?

It seems to me that holidays
with sped up celebrating,
Lack time to ponder everything.
I find it so frustrating

Because if holidays become
Enmeshed in one another,
We'll lose their meaning, lose their joy.
Can't we go back, uncover...

The hidden jewel of family
Who love to be together,
Who come as one, who come in love,
No matter winter weather?

This year please pledge to slow things down,
And savor every minute,
From Halloween to Christmas time
Find joy and love within it.

A KID'S DEFINITION OF LOVE

So tell me, do you want to know the thing most prized by kids?
Then stop, my friend, and listen up, 'cause this is what it is.
Surprisingly, it's not a toy or trip to Disneyland,
It's not that bike they said they'd like, that real expensive brand.

A swimming pool won't make them drool, believe me, that's not
    it.
A trampoline, you think's their dream? On that the jury's split.
Now, just in case you'd like to ask if I have lost my mind,
That any kid would flip his lid, if ever he would find…

The presents I've described above, you ask, "What's not to like?
They'd be elated, shout hooray! You'd tell me, "Take a hike!"
I understand and if I'd scanned that list and I was you,
I'd look around until I found what must be my loose screw.

But hear me out, what it's about, is YOU, my friend, yes, YOU.
That kid of yours knows that the stores are stocked and yes, it's
    true,
And though you think he'd love from you each trinket, toy and
    trip,
Just strip away the words I say, it's YOU they need, you're it!

Your PRESENCE not your PRESENTS is what your kids need
    most.
The time you spend's a dividend and yields a bond that's close.
The times you shared will show you cared, to miss 'twould be a
    crime,
For things, you know, they come and go, but LOVE it
    equals…TIME.

IT'S THE WEEK BEFORE CHRISTMAS

It's a week before Christmas and all through the house
We both are relaxing, just me and my spouse.
The tree lights are sparkling, the stockings are hung,
The cards needing one thing, the lick of a tongue.

The gifts are all purchased, selected online,
From jewelry to toys, to clothing and wine.
What's more, they're all wrapped, boy, am on the ball!
It's time to start baking…but the clock on the wall…

Says, "Hey, listen, it's midnight, it's bedtime, you Silly,
After all you've been racing around willy-nilly.
Just stop for a minute, look at all that you've done.
C'mon get some rest now, you've accomplished a ton!"

Besides there's tomorrow, another day dawns.
Right now my beds calling, I'm responding with yawns.
Tomorrow I'll get up and promise I'll be
Relaxed and less frantic, I've a week more, you see…

To do all my baking, read cards, do some calling,
With personal wishes, those visits, enthralling.
For it's easy to get all caught up in preparing
And forget that the season's a time meant for sharing.

It doesn't revolve 'round the presents, the baking,
But rather that Baby, God's love for the taking.
It's easy to get all caught up in the doing,
Forgetting what happened that gave hearts renewing.

We've just got to stop, take a moment to ponder
The meaning of Christmas, lest it's meaning we squander.
No matter your project, God gives enough time
To do what's important whether yours, whether mine.

This holiday season cherish loved ones and say,
"God's Son is the reason we have Christmas day.
All else doesn't matter if we have only this,"
Then close with, "I love you" and seal with a kiss.

FOR YOU AND ALL THE EARTH

"Oh, Christmas is for children,"
Or so the saying goes.
Such happy faces, sounds of glee,
Ol' Santa's bright, red nose!

But also it's the time we spend
With family and friends,
The flickering candles, trees so bright,
The cards we like to send.

But what about the Christmas Child
Born on that star-lit night?
The awe-struck shepherds, overwhelmed,
To see that wondrous sight!

Why is it that we put aside
What we should not forget?
How is it we're consumed instead
About what we'll regret?

For isn't it of worldly things
That we should all be wary?
Is buying this and buying that
What makes our Christmas merry?

My friend, it's not the tinsel, tree,
The presents wrapped in splendor,
Not carols by the fireside,
No, it's the Babe so tender.

Oh, yes, indeed, that tiny Babe
Was born to set men free!
God's grace and love were born that night,
Yes, born for you and me.

So as you shop and wrap and cook
For guests that you're expecting,
Remember why we celebrate.
Make sure you're not rejecting...

The reason for this holiday.
'Twas Jesus' humble birth.
Yes, He was born that holy night
For you and all the earth.

'TWAS THE DAY AFTER CHRISTMAS

'Twas the day after Christmas
When all through the land
There was pushing and shoving
With an elbow or hand.

The crowds before Christmas
Sought out bargains galore,
Now, too, on a mission
Knocked things to the floor.

They were thinking of next year,
Buying paper and bows
And cards for the sending,
With love, I suppose.

It wasn't Black Friday
But resembled the chaos.
The shoppers were yelling,
"We were first, c'mon take us!"

The more that they waited,
The louder their chatter.
Disregarding all others,
Thinking only they mattered.

Seeing all this first-hand,
I thought about Christmas,
Found my spirits start sagging
From this out-of-whack business!

Had no one remembered
What the season had meant?
The love of the Christ-child
Had it come and then went?

Or worse had their Christmas
Lacked love from the start,
A mere get-together,
Not been from the heart?

Was it all about presents
Most expensive, most prized?
What a sad commentary,
This Christmas of lies.

"Dear Father in heaven,
Look down from above.
Your children are straying.
Please, bring back the love ...

Of Bethlehem's Jesus
So tender and mild,
Who came to this earth
As a baby, your child.

They've forgotten what happened
On that first Christmas day.
They've forgotten your Son, Lord,
Whose the Truth and the Way."

On this day after Christmas
Let's remember the reason,
That it's not about bargains,
Or our gifts for next season.

Hold sacred the birthday
Of Jesus our King,
The BEST gift of Christmas,
Above everything!

Andrew McDowell became interested in writing at age 11, and by the time he was 13, he knew he wanted to be a writer. He is the author of the epic fantasy novel *Mystical Greenwood*. He has also written and published short stories, poetry, and creative nonfiction. Andrew studied at St. Mary's College and the University of Maryland, College Park. He is a member of the Maryland Writers' Association. He was diagnosed with Asperger syndrome, an autism spectrum disorder, when he was 14. Visit andrewmcdowellauthor.com to learn more about him and his writing.

HARVEST'S END

Bounty gathered at harvest's end.
Fruits from our labor ripe and fat,
Celebrate now with every friend.

All that we tenderly attend,
Protected from crow or the rat,
Bounty gathered at harvest's end.

Light fires as the days descend.
Past ghostly trend and the black cat,
Celebrate now with every friend.

Wintertime just around the bend,
Put on a warm coat and a hat.
Bounty gathered at harvest's end.

Together we shall not offend.
Relatives we hug, pets we pat.
Celebrate now with every friend.

Giving thanks to what life did send.
Driving always from this to that.
Bounty gathered at harvest's end.
Celebrate now with every friend.

QUIET LEAVES

Each has shriveled in passing time.
Having lost their midsummer prime,
One by one they have fallen to the ground.

In autumn they can all be seen.
Very few are still a bright green.
They are scattered in great heaps all around.

Quietly they all waste away,
Like refuse tossed out yesterday,
Splendor once gone they shall never regain.

Forgotten thus each left its mark,
Where others will bud from the bark,
Until such a time, this silence shall reign.

WINTER BIRDS TO BEHOLD

So many winter birds to behold
When south all others have gone away
Only a few can withstand the cold
Like the cardinal and the blue jay

When south all others have gone away
Unto my snowbound backyard they flew
Like the cardinal and the blue jay
By far these were my favorite two

Unto my snowbound backyard they flew
Grackles and starlings love to harass
By far these were my favorite two
To scare away by banging the glass

Grackles and starlings love to harass
All those willing to share as they feed
To scare away by banging the glass
For them I have left each single seed

All those willing to share as they feed
Only a few can withstand the cold
For them I have left each single seed
So many winter birds to behold

WINTER HOLIDAYS

When there has fallen the darkest of night,
Underneath thick clouds or a starry dome,
All are gathered in search of warming light.

From far and wide so many souls did roam,
Yet now with snowfall or winds blowing cold,
We come together to the hearth and home.

Customs observed from generations old,
Whether by candles or beneath great trees,
We feast and we sing and stories are told.

Sharing and making all of these memories,
In this time of year when short are these days,
No matter what your creed, remember please:

Diverse and alike snows fall and flames blaze,
For thence we mark our winter holidays.

THE CHRISTMAS HEARTH

Going home in the cold of snow
With only the lamplight's dim glow
There awaits a warm, friendly blaze
For these are the darkest of days

You know soon you can find rest
Like a winter bird in the nest
Afore the hearth in all its might
Away from the frost in the night

The door is shut and down you plop
Now the snow may heavily drop
You are at home warm and content
Every single worry has spent

Garlands and stockings have been hung
Your cold hands so hard have you rung
Relax now on this Christmas Eve
Until bound for bed you will leave

Can there be a more perfect way
To spend at the end of this day
The hearth will warm body and heart
Not yet will you have to depart

Linda M. Crate's poetry, short stories, articles, and reviews have been published in a myriad of magazines both online and in print. She has twelve published chapbooks: *A Mermaid Crashing Into Dawn* (Fowlpox Press - June 2013), *Less Than A Man* (The Camel Saloon - January 2014), *If Tomorrow Never Comes* (Scars Publications, August 2016), *My Wings Were Made to Fly* (Flutter Press, September 2017), *splintered with terror* (Scars Publications, January 2018), *More Than Bone Music* (Clare Songbirds Publishing House, March 2019), *the samurai* (Yellow Arrowing Publishing, October 2020), *Follow the Black Raven* (Alien Buddha Publishing, July 2021), *Unleashing the Archers* (Guerilla Genesis Press, August 2021), *Hecate's Child* (Alien Buddha Publishing, November 2021) *fat & pretty* (Dancing Girl Press, June 2022), and s*earching stained glass windows for an answer* (Alien Buddha Press, December 2022), and three micro-chapbooks *Heaven Instead* (Origami Poems Project, May 2018), *moon mother* (Origami Poems Project, March 2020), *and & so I believe* (Origami Poems Project, April 2021). She is also the author of the novella *Mates* (Alien Buddha Publishing, March 2022). She also published her debut photography collection *Songs of the Creek* (Alien Buddha Press, April 2023) in spring of 2023.

GROW TO LEARN

mashed potatoes
and gravy,
turkey,
and my favorite: stuffing—

these are the things
i enjoy when i am visiting
family for thanksgiving;

pumpkin pie with whipped
topping and sugar cookies

are welcome treats, too—

if there is pumpkin roll
then i will need a slice of that,

but my favorite is spending
time with family and growing a
closer bond and learning more
about them;

because you can never know a
person fully but you can grow to learn
more about them if you listen.

A BLESSING

normally,
i am working
thanksgiving;

last year was a nice
change of pace

got my first thanksgiving
off so i could celebrate
with my family—

i was grateful because
the customers at work
can be pretty terrible
and especially demanding
when the holidays roll
around as if their poor planning
is somehow my issue and not theirs,

and i tire of people saying to
be grateful i have a job when i
am being abused by customers
left and right because somehow
it is okay to lose your manners
as a grown-up and act like an entitled
toddler over the mildest of
inconveniences—

sometimes a job is just a job
which affords you to pay the bills,
and that's all this is;

but i am grateful to have a roof
over my head and clean water to drink—

i know i am blessed,
yet my job is full of stress;
so any holiday i have off that i can
have and spend time with my family
is a blessing.

ALL I CARE ABOUT

i prefer
the years when
i don't have to
work christmas,

i love to spend time
at home with family;

instead of having to deal
with rude and demanding
customers who have no
understanding and only have
a sense of entitlement and need
even on christmas—

one christmas at work
a drunkard got mad at me
because i told him we weren't
open yet,

asked me if i knew what it was
like to be an alcoholic instead of
being grateful for my kindness;

and i pray that i never have so
little family and friends that i become
that way—

let me sit beneath the christmas tree
with my mother, my sister, my sister's
boyfriend, the dog fizzy,
and my dad if he isn't called
out to plow the snow;
and let us watch movies and open gifts—

let us eat cookies and enjoy the
warmth of family and love,
that's all i care about.

THE BEST GIFT

autumnal and winter
gatherings with family
and friends are my
favorite,

sweeter than the iced sugar
cookies or chocolates
we indulge in;

love is a gift of magic
that i have never taken for granted—

unwrapping smiles
and joy,
when i see that i've given
them a thoughtful gift they
appreciate warms my heart;

the laughter and joy
of this little moments
takes up space
in my heart—

because the best gift is time
spent with those whom we love.

THE MOST MAGICAL GIFT

i love to be home
for christmas,
it's always been a big
holiday in our house;

the tree is always
sparkling and bright
full of light—

gifts are always opened
in the morning,
but i am always just happiest
to be there and to be included;

smells of cookies and green
bean casserole in the air—

the chocolate covered cherries
are my favorite because i
love cherries and i love chocolate
so what better combination is there than this?

when i open my eyes
on christmas morning,
witness the tree and all the gifts
lovingly tucked with care;

my heart is happy because
love is the most magical gift able
to warm the heart years later.

Catherine A. MacKenzie's writings are found in numerous print and online publications. She writes all genres but invariably veers toward the dark—so much so her late mother once asked, "Can't you write anything happy?" (She can!)

She published her first novel, *Wolves Don't Knock,* in 2018, and *Mister Wolfe (*the darkly dark second) in 2020. Two volumes of grief poetry commemorate her late son Matthew: *My Heart Is Broken* and *Broken Hearts Can't Always Be Fixed*. She has also published other books of poetry and short story compilations, all available on Amazon or from her.

Cathy divides her time between West Porters Lake and Halifax, Nova Scotia, Canada.

She can be followed at http://writingwicket.wordpress.com

PERPETUAL FAMILY CHRISTMAS

We gather 'round the table to feast on roast turkey,
dressing/stuffing (mine's the world's best), creamy mashed
potatoes (your fav), sliced sweet potatoes, mushy peas (no
one's fav),

After we're stuffed, we dig into pumpkin pies topped with
whipped cream, as well as fruitcake and plum pudding with
custard sauce,

There was wine and beer throughout the afternoon and evening,
along with assorted chocolates wrapped in colourful foil,
numerous snacks, appetizing appetizers,

Your funeral candle's the table's centrepiece, flanked by greenery
and angels, lit shortly before we sat,

Did you see the flickering flame?

Forever, for as long as I breathe, that empty chair will remain.
Call me a crazy old senile mother, but I'll always pretend you
sit beside me at Christmas, enjoying mashed taters and sliced
turkey, topped with overflowing gravy.

(Previously published in *Broken Hearts Can't Always Be Fixed*, March 2022.)

CAROLS DON'T ALWAYS RHYME

Christmas time
Carols that rhyme
Weather cold
Snowflakes bold

Fruitcake
To bake
Pumpkin pie
Turkey to buy

Trimmings
And brimmings
Flavoured coffee
And toffee

Turkey stuffing
Santa puffing
After his feed
Oh, such greed!

Tree stands tall
In the hall
Ornaments bright
In the night

I inhale pine
All that's fine
But something's amiss
In this abyss

With Matt gone
On that dawn
Living without my lad
Days are sad

I think of him always
My eyes ablaze
Drinking beers
With tears

Life goes on
No matter a yawn
Or the whys
And cries

His chair is here
Along with a beer
Matt, if you're free
Please come see

Come 'round
Sit down
We'll pretend
Life doesn't end

(Previously published in *Broken Hearts Can't Always Be Fixed*, March 2022.)

THE EMPTY CHAIR

Never fear, Mom, I'll be there,
So set out that cold cold beer;
I won't miss your marvellous meal,
Not at Christmas, a serious deal
With family, exchanging presents,
Breathing in yuletide scents;
Move the chairs tight together
As if huddled in frigid weather,
But leave an empty chair for me,
Please, thank you, I beg and plea.

You may not see me but I'll see you,
So enjoy the day, don't be blue;
I'm the ornament shining bright
On the tree day and night,
I'm the star behind the day
And the light hiding the grey,
I'm the dark around the moon,
The laughter within the tune;
I'll be in that chair saved for me,
Sharing my jokes, pranks, and glee.

I don't want you to mourn;
Yes, I was conceived and born,
Lived and tragically died,
And, Mom, oh how I tried
To stay, to grasp a breath
That'd save me from death;
I miss everyone every day
And wish I'd been able to stay;
Though it's more than you can bear
Please leave that empty chair.

I couldn't thwart my calling
Despite all your bawling,
Your tears and your fears;
I had thirty-six good years
And appreciate all you did;
Though sometimes I badly slid
And you weren't always proud,
Didn't I stand out in a crowd?
I'm fine, don't pine, save me
That chair at the table by the tree.

Christmas is huge in my new home,
The place where I now roam;
It's not bad, not what you might think;
We talk, laugh and cry, we drink,
So set out four Bud Light
And I'll try with all my might
To leave you a meaningful sign:
Hidden beer cans or a thing of mine,
And while I sit in that empty chair
Remember me fondly in prayer.

I'll drink those four beers
For each of the past four years,
I'll swig heartily and join your toast
Despite being a geeky ghost;
Remember me as jolly as Nick
And light my funeral candle wick;
See the flame winking and blowing?
That's me, slyly grinning and glowing;
You won't see me, but I'll be there
Seated in that empty chair.

(Previously published in *Broken Hearts Can't Always Be Fixed,* March 2022.)

43

SILENCE

Another Christmas, the fifth death's draped you...

Is that you in the far distance, weeping, whimpering, whispering?

Is that your shadow, the form you once were before cancer crept and clutched?

Or is it a caricature, an imposter, a mirage?

I pray it's the spirit of you returned to play pranks, to comfort.

I call out: *Matthew, Matthew, Matthew*...

Alas, silence sits beside me, and farther afield in the cold cheerless night that's not yet dawn—that dreaded dawn that took you before your time as if in our weariness we'd not immediately know—the void festers and flourishes...

I wipe away tears but I'm alone so sunglasses are unnecessary to camouflage mourning—the lugubrious life sentence living with me 'til the day I die and depart,

If you should miraculously return from Heaven for a visit, whether make-believe or mirage-y, let's pretend the reunion is real, that life never ends. That you still breathe...

(Previously published in *Broken Hearts Can't Always Be Fixed,* March 2022.)

Celjoy P. Catapang was born on June 14, 2002, in Tanauan City, Batangas, Philippines. She is a twenty-one-year-old student at Batangas State University, Philippines. She is currently in her last two semesters of her bachelor's degree as a Secondary Education Major in English. She is an aspiring writer who finds writing essays and poetry as an escape to reality and as a tool to express her emotions, feelings, and experiences. She writes things that she experienced or imagined in her life; as a gateway out of boredom; and a great way for learning and improving.

As an inspiring literary artist, you can check her works in the previous anthology *A Children's Book of Bedtime Verse* published by Southern Arizona Press, available on Amazon.

IN BETWEEN

I am in between —
In between of those memories
Memories, I've long for —
Etched in my mind,
But I can't make it happen twice.

I am in between —
In between of longing and hoping —
Or just longing but not expecting
I know I can't,
But honestly it's the word "I couldn't".

I am in between —
Torn between wanting or it's me needing.
I am needy one, wanting for some —
Some chance for us
That moment, first and last.

I am in between —
I couldn't help but bring back;
Bring back those chances we had.
The clock says "tick tock";
Time is running, please knock.

I am in between —
Between the seasons of autumn or spring.
The season of winter,
Like snows falling;
Tears can't help but showing.

I am in between —
Staying or going back.
This winter season, family is a must.
In a cold winter night,
With my scarf, I want their warmth.

SNOWDROP

In the darkest and coldest time, be a flower —
A flower which blooms under the falling snow that showers.
Flower the blooms gracefully, signifies peace and new beginnings;
A flower that has its own timing.

In this darkest and coldest time, under the falling icy snows;
Putting ours arms together, with hugs and kisses in our thick
    clothes.
Like snowdrop flowers, they bloom altogether;
Family is like a flower, stand tall amidst this weather.

In this darkest and coldest time, there is light and joy
Celebrating holidays with family, a must to enjoy.
Singing carol of the bells or jingle bell rock,
And putting treats on each other's socks.

In this coldest season of the year
You're a flower but nothing to fear.
You are with a family, surely this is another new beginning;
A chapter to enjoy even the year is ending.

In this holiday, you are a not a flower alone;
You are amongst with flowers, supporting each other in this
    winter season.
Through thick and thin in this winter holidays
Family blooms gracefully every hour and every day.

WARM HOLIDAY IN A CHILLY DAY

It is the time of the year where puddles become transient skating
    rinks
Hands at the pocket, playing with smoke-like vapor coming from
    our mouths.
It's holiday, houses are full of drinks
House is a home; I can feel its warmth.

Everyone is all smiles at the door
Clasping their hands in delight
Twinkling eyes, waiting for more
A time of the year, completed, what a sight.

Kids start to play,
making snowballs at their hands
Wanting it to make it bigger, molding it like clay.
"Catch it" in your face, it lands.

The adults busied themselves.
Talking with each other,
With unending hugs and kisses
And this will continue until later.

Put my hands, palm to palm.
Warmth caused by a friction, I guess so.
I thank the Heavens, this feels homely warm.
No scientific explanation, warmth is family amidst snow.

WARMTH

Winter is the season to celebrate;
Amidst plunging temperature, let's still wait.
Radiant and shining in those scarves and mittens.
Magical and magnificent like a snowball in the foyer.
Tranquility amongst loud cheers and laughter,
Home is where you are, my family, forever.

Marianne Tefft is a poet and voice-over reader who daylights as a Montessori teacher in Sint Maarten. Her poems and short stories have appeared in print, online and on air in North America, Europe, Asia, and the Caribbean. She is the author of the poetry anthologies *Full Moon Fire: Spoken Songs of Love* and *Moonchild: Poems for Moon Lovers*.

THE WARMTH OF SNOW

I wake into deep silence
Paining my ears for sounds of life
Even the neighborhood dogs are in remission
The green desert still cowers from the urgent sun
I am longing for the warmth of the snow

CHRISTMAS LIGHTS

Overhead pendants of holiday lights
Flow between high-rise towers
Lustrous strands of Carnival beads
Strive to brighten the Long Night Moon
Like unnatural raindrops
That trace sturdy veins
And settle into the cupped palms
Of verdant elephant's ears
After December rain

CHRISTMAS STAR

You squint into a light
They call the Christmas Star
You might be tempted to recall its bright birth
And stumble as you walk in the glare
Of the tempests tsunamis vile tides and genocides
Over which its brilliance has been called to preside
But that small Sun is not a gazing ball
Neither mirror nor glowing haruspex
In which to ruminate about all that is gone
Instead like them it rests upon your horizon
To focus your attention not on what is past
But to urge you to ask
What will you do next

BOXING DAY

Among the sharp needles
Slivers from a frail bulb
Shattered on red tile
Shards of love
Tinsel dulled
Scattered forlorn
Awaiting the broom

Melanie D. Nora, a 22-year-old Filipino student who is pursuing a Bachelor degree of Secondary Education Major in English at Batangas State University TNEU - JPLPC Malvar Campus, Philippines. She previously held a position as a media specialist for their department organization, "The Chatterbox Society." As a student, she believes that having a variety of interests will help her to grow as a person and enhance her skills and abilities as a future educator. Also, she believes that if she's dedicated to her profession, she is capable of and motivated to impart knowledge and inspire those around her, especially her future students.

SHADES OF GREEN

Each hue represents differences.
Each color shows different emotions.
Yet when I think of green, I think about christmas.

Twas the dark that reminds me of hue
And 'twas the season saved me from that blue.
Twas the sage when I think of my life
And 'twas the season saved me from that time.

Twas the peppermint tea that makes me grounded
And 'twas my blanket saved me from that cold.
Twas the pine when I realized, the season has begun
And 'twas the gifts under the tree reminds me of childhood.

HOLIDAY RUSH

Riding in a vintage galant
From provinces to cities
Looking for a place to stay
And thinking not to get lost.

Rain starts to sing
Yet there's no place to stay.
Begin to feel hopeless
But there's no turning back.

Looking for signs and symbols
Then the fog starts to be visible.
The adrenaline starts to rush
'Til there's a light from a house in the distance.

There's a lot of folks celebrating
They're enjoying the momentum
Children are happy to open their gifts
As others enjoyed their hot coffee and read books.

The lady said, "there's one small room left"
Still deciding whether to check in or not.
The clock is ticking, the pen is clicking.
'Til she gave the keys for the room.

Sighs –
"Finally!"

Feel the sense of peace amidst the noise outside
Looking at the window pane
And spellbound by the beauty of the jiffy
While listening to Billie Holiday's song, "Easy Living."

MAZE

She wake up from some sort of illusion
And everything seems to be perfect.
Start to wonder where's that collection
'Til she's weary of finding it.

Christmas countdown begin
Stores starts to sell christmas decors
Children are ready to write their wishes
And starts to play the violin.

Winter season is approaching
Everyone seems to be excited
But finding it is still hard
Searching everywhere yet there's no sign of showing.

Relatives from the city have arrived
But it is still can not be found
Everyone start to help looking for it
One box left and hoping for it.

Wishing, praying, and thinking where it
could be? "I might have lost it?"
Is she still in her own world?
Sighs, "what will I do?"
And the clouds start to fade.

Remember where it could be
Starts to climb up to the tree house
Till she found a blue box full of dust
Cheeks turning red and eyes seem too bright.

Surroundings start to look vivid
Reminiscing those moments
Singing, dancing, and making apple pies.
And the realization strikes
Those moments are still in the photo album.

THOUSAND MILES

Picture-perfect smile that drew over lots of hearts
And provides a sense of security and sunlight.
In arms that welcomed my imperfection and became my favorite.
It was a reminiscence for me to hold onto.

The time has come, the season has begun.
Can smell the aroma of spicy cinnamon.
Candles are dripping, musty scent and pumpkins look great
And it starts to get colder.

Every year, we're excited to visit them.
I still remember how you plan to prepare things
Organize here, organize there
And it became a little tradition.

I wonder how you feel about your new home
Is it safe there? Is it cozy there?
It's my turn to get things ready like you always do
As you're already a thousand miles away.

How does it feel to lie in that bed?
Is it soft? Is it comfortable?
You become one of them, lie in bed peacefully
Give flowers, light a candle, and say a little prayer for your
    happiness.

Ram Krishna Singh, also known as R.K.Singh, has been writing for over four decades now . Born (31 December 1950), brought up and educated in Varanasi, he has been professionally concerned with teaching and research in the areas of English language teaching, especially for Science and Technology, and Indian English Poetry practices.Until the end of 2015, Professor of English (HAG) at IIT-ISM in Dhanbad, Dr Singh has published 56 books, including poetry collections *Tainted With Prayers/Contaminado con oraciones* (English/Spanish, 2019), *Silencio: Blanca desconfianza: Silence: White distrust* (Kindle, Spanish/English, 2021), *A Lone Sparrow* (English/Arabic, e-book, 2021), *Against the Waves: Selected Poems* (2021), *Changing Seasons: Selected Tanka and Haiku* (English/Arabic, e-book, 2021), 白濁: *SILENCE: A WHITE DISTRUST* (English/Japanese, Kindle Edition/Paperback, 2021), *SHE: Haiku Celebrating Woman That Makes Man Complete* (e-book, 2022), *Drifty Silence* (e-book, 2023), and *Poems and Micropoems* (Southern Arizona Press, 2023, available on Amazon at https://www.amazon.com/Poems-Micropoems-Ram-Krishna-Singh/dp/1960038087). The poet's poems also appear in the anthologies *Love Letters in Poetic Verse* (ed. Paul Gilliland, 2023) and *Beyond the Sand and Sea* (ed. Paul Gilliland, 2023). His haiku and tanka have been internationally read, appreciated, and translated into over 30 languages.

Find him on Twitter @profrksingh
and on Facebook www.facebook.com/profrksingh .
More at: https://pennyspoetry.wikia.com/wiki/R.K._Singh.
email: profrksingh@gmail.com

LET'S MEET

Before the bananas ripe
let's meet at least once

lest the fog dampen passion
let's water our love

the sun is bright this morning
and night's promising

let's meet and unfreeze winter
of years, drink some wine

restore warmth of faith and hope
and heal the breaches

without black goggles for seeing
let's meet at least once

(From my collection *You Can't Scent Me and Other Selected Poems* (New Delhi: Authors Press, 2016, p.17)

LOVE'S NARROW PASSAGE:
A HAIKU SEQUENCE

Clad in white
peaks behind peaks-
everest within

too inviting
her curvier lines-
decollete dress

sweet perfume
untainted flower
evening lust

he sleep-babbles
let's become earth and sky:
five-decade love

adventure
between the thighs-
tailored deal

she wrings her hair
rising from the lake:
rural venus

part of me
enters her body:
blooms puffball

seated woman
sleepy gestures
dim delight

she wanted to sing
dream-songs she couldn't:
spring hand-cuffed

a curled snake
with fangs ready to poison
love's narrow passage

AGAINST THE WAVES

The crowded lift and emptiness of the flat
doesn't help me resurrect what's gone

late at night I may pile hopes on a pale paper
trying to invent a new life to live with

end up seized by pain trolling in the shady light
double bed, blank mirror, and still greyer dawn

the pillow hurts, the image derides, the prayers fail
the roaring inside, the ghostly silence

and unfading darkness. I'm no Odysseus
but keep straying against the waves

(From my collection *Against the Waves: Selected Poems* (New Delhi: Authors
Press, 2021, p. 23)

Lynn White lives in north Wales. Her work is influenced by issues of social justice and events, places, and people she has known or imagined. She is especially interested in exploring the boundaries of dream, fantasy, and reality. She was shortlisted in the Theatre Cloud 'War Poetry for Today' competition and has been nominated for a Pushcart Prize, Best of the Net, and a Rhysling Award. Her poetry has appeared in many publications including: *Apogee, Firewords, Capsule Stories, Gyroscope Review,* and *So It Goes.* This is her ninth appearance in a Southern Arizona Press anthology.

Find Lynn at:

https://lynnwhitepoetry.blogspot.com
https://www.facebook.com/Lynn-White-Poetry-1603675983213077/

CHRISTMAS CROW

We watched the crow with fascination
as it tap tapped on the window pane,
saw its black eyes gleaming,
its wet feathers shining
in the moonlight.
And we understood.

We understood that it wanted to join us,
to perch amongst the baubles
on our shining tree
to share our fireside warmth
on Christmas Eve
and escape
the cold winter rain.

We heard it promise
to sing for us
We opened the window
and let it in.
It crowed a Christmas carol.

First published in *Third Wednesday Magazine*, Winter 2021

FATHER CHRISTMAS

I was so excited.
It was nearly Christmas
and I was going to meet
Father Christmas himself.

I was so excited,
wearing my best coat and bonnet,
hopping from one foot to the other
in the long queue of children
waiting with their mums
to be allowed into Santa's Grotto.

I was so excited.
We were nearly there.
I could see the grotto
with it's tinsel and fairy lights
twinkling.
I was going to sit on his knee
and have my picture taken,
and that was in an age when
photographs were even rarer
than Christmases..

I was so excited.
There were the elves...
But wait..
they were cardboard.
Where were the real elves,
the magic ones,
why weren't they there?
"They're much too busy",
my mum said.
"But Father Christmas will be real".

We paid our money
and there he was.
He really was.
I couldn't wait to climb on his knee
and examine his beard.
I'd never seen a beard before.
But he was very tetchy when I pulled at it
and told me to stop.
Then it went lop sided
and I realised
it was a false beard
and I told him so, angrily.
He put it back.
"Stop thy wriggling", he said.
"You're not the real one,
I don't want to sit on your knee"

Flash went the camera.

And outside there was a queue of children
waiting
to be addressed.
Hands on hips.
"He's not the real one.
He's got a false beard.
He's not magic at all,
they're cheating you!"
It's a swiz!
Then the store manager came..

I was so excited.

First published in *Me As A Child Series* by Silver Birch Press, May 2015

CHRISTMAS TREE

Trimming the tree was a Christmas Eve ritual
in my family.
Each year my cousin would come to help my mum.
They would carefully take the glass baubles from the box
that used to hold her big doll called Topsy.
Then they would put them all in their special place
in my family.
"No the elephant doesn't go there,
that's where the peacock should be
and the Christmas pudding goes above."
Everything had it's place on the Christmas tree
in my family.

There were shiny miniature crackers never to be pulled
and curly, coloured candles never to be lit, for economy.
No tinsel was allowed for that was cheating.
Only baubles to cover the tree, hiding the green.
The glass baubles had belonged to my cousin,
so had the tree. And earlier, to her mother and granny,
all in my family.
The only family to fall out over trimming a tree,
my cousin's husband used to say with some truth,
as every year the arguments as to which
bauble should go where were replayed
in my family.

So much stress over trimming a Christmas tree,
that I think they drank Santa's sherry!
They must have needed it!
And ate his mince pies,
after trimming the tree
in my family.

First published in *Me In The Holidays Series* by Silver Birch Press, December 2015

Dr. Nora V. Marasigan is a Filipino associate professor in the undergraduate teacher education programs at Batangas State University JPLPC-Malvar. As an educator, she is primarily interested in conducting studies on mathematics and mathematics education which focus on topics essential to educational innovations. She has been invited as a resource speaker in seminars/webinars dealing with Mathematics teaching and learning, test construction, and analyzing research data. She is a mathematics professor and has published research articles on mathematics, mathematics education, and pedagogy in an international peer-reviewed journal. She has also published creative works in a multidisciplinary academic publisher and won the Best Poetry and Best Short Story Awards in the Cape Comorin Writers' Festival 2020.

AUTUMN'S FAMILY FEAST

As leaves of amber and gold descend,
To family, our hearts and hands extend.
In the autumn's embrace, we come together,
For a feast of love, in any weather

The table is set with dishes galore,
From generations past, recipes we adore.
A cornucopia of flavors to savor and share,
As we gather 'round, a family affair.

From pumpkin pies to turkey's grace,
In fall's abundance, we find our place.
With gratitude and love, we fill each plate,
In the company of family, we celebrate.

The crisp air echoes with laughter's sound,
As leaves carpet the ground all around
In autumn's warmth, we find our way,
To celebrate family on this special day

EMBRACING LOVE IN WINTER'S GRACE

In winter's gentle, icy hold,
We gather close, the young and old.
With snowflakes dancing, cold and bright,
We celebrate this wondrous night.

With hearthside warmth and love aglow,
We share our stories, hearts all aflow.
The season's magic, pure and true,
In our hearts, it's always anew.

The twinkling lights on evergreens,
Create a world of stunning scenes.
In winter's grace, we find our way,
To celebrate this special day

As snow blankets the world in white,
We celebrate with pure delight.
In winter's arms, we find our grace,
Embracing love in this cold place.

FAMILY'S EMBRACE

As winter's chill begins to play,
We gather close on this special day.
In the warmth of family's embrace,
The holidays bloom with love and grace.

Around the table, we all convene,
Faces familiar, like a cherished scene
Laughter and stories, we freely share,
In this circle of love, nothing can compare.

Through frosty windows, we see the snow,
But inside, the warmth continues to grow.
In the heart of winter, we find our way,
Celebrating together, come what may.

With hugs and smiles, we celebrate,
The love that binds, it's never too late.
In winter's cold, our hearts stay warm,
In the arms of family, we weather the storm.

Victoria Puckering, goes by the name of Toria and the Naked Poet. Her work has been described as naked and raw. She lives in Yorkshire, England.

She writes original poetry of all genres and has only been writing for about four years. Her poems have been podcasted in New York, USA and Drystone radio, Yorkshire, England and also various poetry sites on Facebook.

Last year, she became a published Poetess. Her poetry has contributed to the following anthologies:

The Poppy: A Symbol of Remembrance, The Wonders of Winter, Castles and Courtyards, Beyond the Sand and Sea, and *A Children's Book of Bedtime Verse* published by Southern Arizona Press; *Encore Anthology* by Jimmy Broccoli as well as The Dark Poetry Society anthologies and Wheelsong Poetry.

CHRISTMAS EVE

It must be Christmas
American Christmas movies on TV
These American movies are so cheesy
They are sparkly and bright
Everything turns out all right
This is an American Christmas
They have cookies and candy sticks
A love story
The full package
These American movies are too good to be true!
Let's face it you can't beat Scrooge
Starring Alistair Sim
Scrooge is when Christmas truly can begin!
A traditional British Christmas is wonderful
With turkey, Christmas pud, mince pies
Scrooge will always keep our traditions alive!
We watch Scrooge as we eat mince pies and wrap
Christmas presents way into the night
This our Christmas Eve too right!

THE CHRISTMAS BEAT

Wrapping up on Christmas Day
Late again today
Open presents
To the Christmas beat
Vying for a comfy seat
Pigging out on a Christmas feast
Watching the King's speech
Drinking Bucks Fizz and English beer
The Christmas music replayed
Replayed
Coming around again
Like on a carousel
Tummy emptied
Tummy full
Dreaming of endless food
Remembering who bought you what
Like being a contestant on the Generation Game
Christmas presents on the conveyor belt
Remembering every present
I didn't get the cuddly toy
I munch on the candy sweets
Continuing on this Christmas beat
Still vying for the comfiest seat
Still pigging out on the Christmas feast

THE BEAUTIFUL AMAZING GIFT

It is a season of true love
The biggest present is to celebrate with those you love
We are still here today
To celebrate those who have sadly passed away
Never too far from our daily thoughts
Especially on this extra special day
Remember all the laughter, tears, smiles, and just wonderful times
Every day is a present
A gift of life
All the amazing memories we have yet to live
This is the most beautiful, amazing gift

Cynthia Pratt is one of the founding members of the Olympia Poetry Network's board which has been in existence for over 30 years. Her poems have appeared in Crab Creek Review, Raven Chronicles, Feminist Theology Poetry, The Raven's Perch, The Writing Disorder, Poetry Breakfast, and other publications, and will appear in Dreich Magazine (June, 2024 issue), and has been published in the anthologies, *Tattoos on Cedar* (2006), *Godiva Speaks* (2011), two anthologies by the Fusion Collective, *Dancing on the Edges* (2017) and *Garden of the Covid Museum* (2021), as well as in the *Hidden in Childhood* anthology and the anthology by Washington Humanities and Empty Bowl Press, *I Sing the Salmon Home* (2023). Her manuscript, *Celestial Drift,* was published in 2016. She is a former Fish and Wildlife biologist, retiring in 2008. A former Lacey Councilmember and Deputy Mayor of the City of Lacey for the last 12 years, her term ended in December 2021. She is the first Poet Laureate of Lacey as of 2022.

Cynthia grew up in Truckee, California, a town in the Sierra Nevada mountains, just below Donner Summit. Snow season was nine to ten months of the year. She learned to ski at age three and rode sleds down the hill from her house, turning just in time to not slide onto Highway 80. One year it snowed so much, school was closed for two months because the highway was closed between Reno, Nevada and Sacramento, California, and the train snow sheds had collapsed because of the weight of snow turning to ice. Cynthia had the responsibility of shoveling the snow off her roof that year so it wouldn't cave in, so, she has a peculiar relationship with the Christmas season, both loving it, and dreading it each year. She now lives in Lacey, Washington with her husband. They have two children and three grandchildren. There usually isn't snow, just rain. She can be reached at her website: https://www.cynthia-pratt-poet.net/, clicking on the contact page.

CANCELING ONCE MORE

As each ornament was hung by my daughter
and each piece of tinsel thrown randomly by my son,
the fights building to a loud-crowd pandemonium,
I swallowed my after-dinner refreshment and stormed out,
the ultimatum handed down as a lump of coal.
Every year, faithfully, I cancelled Christmas.

Every season, they came into the room, held hostage
by mother scrooge, promising me goodness, kissing
my cheeks, telling me not to cry. It always worked.
Christmas ran its course, as splendid as orange sticks
melting in your mouth.

This knowledge of the past carries weight.
My children recite it to friends, teachers, the tantrum
will be passed down to their grandchildren,
written into genealogical records.
I don't mind. I, too, have passed down
'whimseys' of my parents, grandparents, and husband.

That is why I now think about the weighted announcement,
telling my husband, and grown son it's silly to bother, wait
for the begged for comfort, the laughter to relive my quirky
self, even though the house is empty of young children, chocolate

treats, no quick fixes. I start decorating: nutcracker stocking
     hanger
on the mantle, my homemade Partridge in a Pear Tree decoration
rehung on the wall. Nothing is quite put back together as last
     year
but the void fills no matter what I do.

CHOOSING THE TREE

Height is important:
the trunk tall and straight,
a sturdy, 4-inch point at the top.

When you walk around it,
check the limbs:
each one uniformly
longer than the next,
each side sloping like a well-built barn roof:
narrow, widening, then full at the bottom.

Branch after branch drops
so that the old, blue Christmas balls,
the tinsel and the Cub Scout paper circles
with your child's face can dimple
purposefully above the next tier.

Inspect the needles.
They must prickle yet bend.
Imagine your sister's brush
you used to comb her hair.
As you pull against the fascicles,
check your mitten.
If it is porcupined with needles,
go to the next tree.

But what if that one tree of choice
beacons to you, looking like family:
a little-lopsided, too sparse at the top,
uncontrolled, with a character you understand?
Embrace the asymmetry.
Bring it home like you would your
peculiar cousin you haven't seen
for twenty years.
Let the exotic scent greet the children.

Bedeck the tree in camouflage: extra lights
Aunt May's handmade angel bending down to well-wishers.
Place the 'good side' out toward the neighbors
the way mother taught you.
And while you decorate, don't forget the hot chocolate
and those special orange sticks.
you know the ones,
their sweet-tart taste
always reminds you of home.

CHRISTMAS SEASON IN CAIRO
Egypt, 2004-2005

I.

My daughter's doctor informs her
"Twins,"
something she didn't count on.
She's horrified, at least at first.

But now, Beth tells me
over the broken air waves,
"Resigned." "Will adapt."
"It's okay."

Her German husband is ecstatic,
not realizing how the weight of two
fetuses crush the diaphragm
of the thin-boned,

not yet understanding how they disrupt
holding food down, breathing,
as they grow larger and larger
inside a cage.

We prepare, she and I,
In our own way.
She walks, swaying her baggage
to yoga, let's the housekeeper

take Juliane to play with other families
when energy settles in the dust motes,
lets her openly gay friend, an anomaly
in a Muslim country,

order custom-made nursing pillows
that never arrive.
I double my sewing of baby blankets,
onesies, wash cloths, quilts.

Pack them in a large duffle bag
along with elephant and giraffe mobiles.
Accumulate all the cloth-fitted diapers

she ordered,
horrified the garbage pickers
will sort through her soiled plastic.
David and I proudly buy more luggage.

II.

Every job breaks down into five.
There's the drivers, the door men,
the water cooler men, the fruit hawkers,
newspaper boys at the car windows.

Fixers of everything. Never mind the
housekeeper, now a nanny is added
readying for the twins.
Our daughter isn't allowed to drive,

something about status, and
maybe because she's due.
We never strap in.
Safety is an act of faith.

The Imams' prayer songs mark
The sun's movement,
wakes us at dawn,
shortly after lunch,

late afternoon, after sunset,
nightfall. We need no watch.
Minarets knife the skyline, as frequently
as coffee stands in Olympia.

Later, my daughter tells us
the chants are recorded,
to make sure we don't mistake
necessity with romanticism.

III.

The week runs from Sunday through Thursday.
I'm never sure what day it is.
My son-in-law leaves for work and
my granddaughter, Juliane, for her Irish-run preschool.

Beth dozes, then orders the Company driver
 to drive all of us to ancient architecture, mosques,
Khan el-Kahlili Market, and the Coptic Quarter.
The Great Pyramid reminds us that only the traffic is new.

IV.
We celebrate Christmas, even midnight mass,
watch Juliane's school play. A bearded Muslim Santa
ho, ho's each child on his knee.
Our granddaughter sings,
shyness only temporarily ebbing.

My husband, son, and I go on a cruise up the Nile
visiting temples, the Valley of the Kings.
Still the babies don't arrive,
each now seven pounds and growing.

My daughter sprawls bloated and
gray on the couch,
a stranded, sick whale,
reminding me of flotsam on the Nile shore.
We wait, but then it's time to leave.

David and Brian fly back home,
Then even I must leave. The doctor won't rush
even for large twins and narrow pelvis'.
Maybe we should have stayed home,
reduce their need to entertain.

Twins arrive three days after I return.
cesarean a success.
My son-in-law calls to say everyone is fine.
An Imam's recording chants
the 6 pm prayer in the background
of this happy, blessed New Year.

Karen A. VandenBos was born on a warm July morn in Kalamazoo, Michigan. She has a PhD in Holistic Health where a course in shamanism taught her to travel between two worlds. She can be found unleashing her imagination in two online writing groups and her writing has been published in *Lothlorien Poetry Journal*, *Blue Heron Review*, *The Rye Whiskey Review*, *One Art: a journal of poetry*, *Anti-Heroin Chic*, *The Ekphrastic Review*, *Southern Arizona Press*, *MacQueens's Quinterly*, and others. Karen is a 2024 Best of the Net nominee. This is her fourth appearance in a Southern Arizona Press anthology.

SUGAR & SPICE

Tis the night before Christmas
and all thru my dreams are the
scents of cakes, cookies and cream.

The air tastes of cinnamon, nutmeg
and spice, my mouth is watering,
this dream feels so nice.

I lick chocolate off beaters, lick
fingers and bowls, the sweetness of
sugar invades my soul.

Molasses, vanilla, ginger and salt,
frosting and sprinkles, gum drops
and malt.

Cookies and cake, fudge and pies
I wish my stomach was as big as my
eyes.

Eggs, sugar and milk, mixed with
some flour, a little bit of lemon to
add a wee bit of sour.

Is this really a dream or is it
for real, I'll have to wait and see
what the scale does reveal.

Holidays and baking, oh what a treat.
Merry, merry to everyone, whatever
you eat!

HOME FOR THE HOLIDAYS

Winter shrouds the sky in a scarf of
gray, a pale sun struggles to warm us.
I notice the streetlights flicker as they
come on and I turn my thoughts toward
home.

As the moon rises, the north wind
trumpets through the trees and I
hasten to close the door and light the
yule fire. Soon the carolers will wander
the streets singing their songs of good
tidings and joy.

Tonight the house will be alive with
family and friends, all here to celebrate
the holidays, their faces will be rosy
and the sound of laughter and joy will
permeate the air.

They enter with a swirl of glittering
snow and the scent of cinnamon, their
woolen gloves and hats set to dry on
the hearth. Drinks are poured and
toasts are given, the merriment is
underway.

As midnight drops her weary head we
gather in front of the tree and talk of
the new year to come. We shake the
boxes in their pretty paper and make
up stories of what each one contains.

Soon everyone shuffles off to bed and
I sit with the dying embers of the yule
log. The fragrance of holiday baking
lingers in the worn out pockets of my
apron.

As I look out the window and watch
the softly falling snow, it is then I
realize how grateful I am to be home.

ON CHRISTMAS EVE

Tree lights glisten across the snow blanketed
ground and cardinals with plumes of holiday
red sing hymns while eating seeds of holy
communion.

Tonight angels appear like apparitions where
bodies laid down and spread their wings and
the church bells erupt with the carols of our
youth.

As we snuggle into our robes and gaze into
the yule log fire, we remember the Christmas
eves of our childhood and soon we are longing
for the ghost of Christmas past.

Tonight we will leave a candle burning in
the window, beckoning welcome for all
who are lost and give thanks for the blessings
of home.

Jerri Hardesty lives in the woods of Alabama with husband, Kirk, who is also a poet. They run the nonprofit poetry organization, New Dawn Unlimited, Inc. (NewDawnUnlimited.com). Jerri has had over 600 poems published and has won more than 2000 awards and titles in both written and spoken word poetry. This is her ninth appearance in a Southern Arizona Press anthology.

ALMS

I walked upon the soft and loamy trail
So careless of the spider webs across
I followed song of creek beyond the ridge
Where summer cat tails purr in shifting wind
I tiptoed over mossy lichen rocks
And made my way to algae coated shore
I saw her tiny footprints in the sand
And knelt to leave the package in my coat --
A turkey breast cooked free of skin and bone
Some vegetables and square of sweet cornbread --
And then retreated quickly to the trees.
A glance behind in hopes of catching glimpse
Rewards me with her flash of ruddy fur
Red fox with den of healthy, squirming kits
Will share the family feast this Christmas Day.

Previously published in Ohio Poetry Day, 2009

CHRISTMAS IN EL PASO

Luminarios glow,
Lighting every sidewalk,
Little paper bags of sand
And candle,
But so beautiful
And so much a part
Of memory.
Electric star shines
From the stark peak
Of familiar mountains
Proclaiming Christmas
To the houses below.
It's been there
All my life.
Arm in arm on Scenic Drive,
We gaze out over
The city,
Still our city,
Though so much changed.
We stand beneath
The rocky ravine
Where we climbed
To our first kiss
So long ago.
The street lights are white
Down in Juarez,
Amber in El Paso.
The changing colors clearly
Mark the curving
Rio Grande,
Snaking its way
Through the Valley of the Sun.
The desert is an old friend,
Sand swirling 'round us
In obvious recognition.

Greasewood
Crushed in the hand
Smells like fresh rain.
Fleshy yucca and
Prickly pear
Yield water
To those who know
Their secrets.
Yes,
We went home
For Christmas
This year,
For the first time
In over fifteen years,
And I brought back for you
These few lines,
Just to share,
That something unique
That can only be found
Out there.

Previously published in *Encore*, 2006

NEW YEAR'S EVE 2001

We hit the highway
And head south,
Following her siren song
To Lake Ponchartrain
And beyond.
She waits, curving,
Seductive,
Curled up and around
And lying along the shore,
Legs splayed carelessly
Open toward the Gulf,
Her life's blood
Perpetually flowing out,
Muddy waters
Mixing
With salty seas.
She beckons to us,
All laser cut eyes
And diamond teeth,
Promises spill from her ripe lips
Like strings of Mardi Gras beads
And fake pearls;
She beckons to us,
All confidence and ease
With Bourbon on her breath.
She is the Cajun queen
Parading through her royal streets
All flash and noise and music;
She is fingers snapping,
Hips wagging,
Breasts sagging -- pendulous,
But provocative still --
She is smoke
Rising in rings
And ragged-edged clouds

Like feather masks,
And down beyond Canal Street,
In the Vieux Carre,
Her heart beats,
Beats and throbs
And fills the streets.
Ancient harlot,
Conceived in sin,
She'll only break your heart
But you know that
Going in,
And so we did -- New Year's Eve --
A menage-a-trois,
We three,
You, New Orleans, and me.

Previously published in Poetry Society of Texas Book of the Year, 2006

Maureen C. Carasig-Paiton is a instructor from Bulacan State University- Meneses Campus. Presently she is residing at Malolos, Bulacan. She finished her bachelor's and master's degree at Bulacan State University. Currently she is pursuing her doctorate degree at Baliuag University. She teaches Filipino subject and currently she is designated as Student Teaching Supervisor in Teacher Education Department in the same school where she is teaching. She loves writing and teaching.

She can be contacted through:
e-mail at: maureenpaiton1489@gmail.com
Facebook at : Mauie Carasig Paiton

SEASON OF LOVE

Christmas cheer fills the air,
I journey back with my heart close to me,
Back home, where my memories are kept,
Home of my childhood, where love was implied.

All the trees are adorned with twinkling lights,
Reminding me of where I long to be,
Laughter fills every room in this place
The warmth of family eliminates any gloom.

There is a bright fire burning in the hearth,
This cozy haven will keep you warm this winter,
In the kitchen, the aroma's sweet,
Of cookies and pies, a holiday treat.

I see the faces I've missed so dear,
Gathered around with love and cheer,
Hugs and smiles, in each embrace,
Home for the holidays, a sacred space.

Though time has passed and I've been away,
This feeling of home is here to stay,
For family and love, they never part,
Home for the holidays, it warms the heart.

So let the snow fall, let the wind blow,
I'm home for the holidays, and it's aglow,
With love and laughter, joy unmeasured,
In this home where my heart is truly treasured.

HOME WHERE THE HEART IS

Where the heart is light, at home for the holidays,
Family members also congregate day and night.
A moment for celebration, cheer,
When distant and nearby family meet together.

The air is thick with the aroma of pine needles.
Christmas music fills the stairs as.
Children play and giggle with joy,
adults recall memories without memory.

Gifts are carefully and lovingly packaged,
Additionally, stockings were strung festively.
The table is decorated with holiday brightness.
As near and far relatives meet.

The holidays at home, a time so precious,
when spirits are light and hearts are full.
A moment to treasure, a moment to hold,
a period for both new and old memories.

CHRISTMAS JOY

Christmas morning cheer
Sparkling lights and warm embrace
Gifts of love abound

Irina Tall Novikova is an artist, graphic artist, and illustrator. She graduated from the State Academy of Slavic Cultures with a degree in art and also has a bachelor's degree in design. Her first personal exhibition *My soul is like a wild hawk* (2002) was held in the museum of Maxim Bagdanovich. In her works, she raises themes of ecology. In 2005, she devoted a series of works to the Chernobyl disaster and draws on anti-war topics. The first big series she drew was *The Red Book*, dedicated to rare and endangered species of animals and birds. She writes fairy tales and poems and illustrates short stories. She draws various fantastic creatures including unicorns, animals with human faces, and she especially likes the image of a man - a bird - Siren. In 2020, she took part in Poznań Art Week.

Follow her on:

https://instagram.com/irina369tall?igshid=YmMyMTA2M2Y=

https://m.facebook.com/profile.php?v=photos&lst=100009868569

https://www.instagram.com/irinanov4155/?hl=ru

I'M HOLDING OUT MY HANDS

I'm holding out my hands
to the little deer hiding
in the darkness
of the heavenly fir trees Strict branches
My arms embrace
Yellow lights glow
In the distance, where there is
only winter yesterday ...
I need to walk through the cold,
biting snow
To warm up by the fire ...
Looking closer I see a long
spruce,
Round balls glow on it
Lighting someone's souls on fire
And I stay ...
Your own thoughts fly away like birds
leaving me alone ...
Wrapping myself up in a blanket
someone left behind
I'm waiting for the holiday to
come

GLASS BALLS ON A GOLD SURFACE

Glass balls on a gold surface
They roll without breaking,
Don't view all
What are they doing
And warming my remaining heart on
Thin Christmas tree
They are like a small earthly sphere
Multiplying in the dark pupils ...
The clock hands on the tower froze,
Small hammers strike
Sunny by silver bells
And don't close the box,
This reality
Because Christmas has come ...

HE GAVE ME HIS HEART

He gave me his heart
for the new year
To the sound of the chimes
Sealing it in scarlet beads
On blue velvet
And they rest in thoughts ...
And my happiness seems like a ghost
And I'm afraid to touch him
So that he doesn't melt
Like a snowman
under the headlights of a blue truck

Dr. Sara L. Uckelman is an associate professor of logic and philosophy of language at Durham University. Her short stories, poems, and art are published or forthcoming in *Last Leaves, Manawaker Studio Flash Fiction Podcast, the Martian Wave, Pendemic.ie, Pilcrow & Dagger, Speculatief, Story Seed Vault, Sylvia, Tree & Stone,* and *With Painted Words,* and anthologies published by BCubed Press, Black Hare Press, Exterus, Flame Tree Publishing, Grace & Victory, Hic Dragones, Jayhenge Publications, QueerSciFi, and WolfSinger Publications. She is the co-founder of the reviews site SFFReviews.com, and founder of the small press Ellipsis Imprints.

FINDING THE WAY HOME

My feet are sore
I've lost count of the miles
I've walked and walked again
These streets leading
From nowhere to now here.

Here only becomes home
By walking these miles
Spending this time
Feeling the ground
Beneath my sore feet
Over and over
Again and again
These miles bring me home.

April Garcia was born and raised in South Central Texas, Garcia's passion for writing poetry began in high school. Her work has appeared in multiple anthologies published by the Laurel Crown Foundation of San Antonio, Texas, Southern New Hampshire University, River Paw Press, Southern Arizona Press, and the *Chaos Dive Reunion* anthology by Mutabilis Press. She was included in Northwest Vista College's literary journal *The Lantana Review* as well as a number of online literary magazines including The Penmen Review, Red River Review, and Unlost Journal. Her most recent work appeared in the May 2023 issue of Voices de la Luna of San Antonio, Texas. Garcia is a wife and mother homeschooling four children. She earned her Bachelor of Arts in general studies majoring in poetry from Southern New Hampshire University. She is a member of The Poetry Society of Texas and also enjoys reading, crocheting, hiking, blogging, and traveling. This is her third appearance in a Southern Arizona Press anthology.

AVOCADO SALAD

I stand in my kitchen
—as she stood
in hers—
carefully

dice plump, red tomatoes
—their tangy juices
staining the bamboo cutting board

—cube
creamy avocados,
chop
the chilled
iceberg lettuce.

In a bowl,
I mash
my avocado—
as she did
—sprinkle
with garlic powder,
salt
—drizzle
with oil,
and add
lemon juice
before folding.

The same savory green
Gran prepared
—blending ingredients
in a mingling
satisfying
as the varying personalities
of
aunts, uncles
cousins
gathered around
that old
chipped—and faded
fire engine red
—picnic table
enjoying
avocado salad.

First published by Red River Review 2019

Mark Fleisher's fifth book of poetry – *Knowing When* -- was a finalist for the 2023 New Mexico-Arizona Book Co-op's Best New Mexico poetry publication. His poetry and prose have been have been published in online and print anthologies in the United States, Canada, United Kingdom, Nigeria, Kenya, and India. He received a journalism degree from Ohio University and worked as a reporter and editor at newspapers in upstate New York and Washington, D.C. His time in the United States Air Force included a year in Vietnam as a combat news reporter. He was awarded a Bronze Star for meritorious service. The native of Brooklyn, New York is based in Albuquerque, New Mexico.

THIS SILENT NIGHT

Christmas Eve
stars still,
moon silent,
wind hushed,
falling snowflakes
almost heard
Tracks of rabbits,
deer, maybe coyote,
embedded without
a whisper
on white blankets
Holiday lights
blurred by stealthy frost
on opaque window panes
All sound suspended
in midnight chill
except for boys and girls
struggling to stay awake
so they may greet Santa
or Saint Nick and their
trove of holiday presents

A BITTERSWEET CHRISTMAS

She put up the tree
a sturdy, freshly-cut
Scotch pine bought
from the farmer fella
up on Highway 47

Lights carefully strung
ornaments positioned
on welcoming boughs
an angel secured at the top

He seemed confused
when she beckoned him
to come and look
Put it out on the curb,
he said, they'll pick it up
and take it away because
Christmas was over
a few weeks ago

Her eyes could not contain
tears that welled and a few
slowly rolled down her cheeks
He has no idea why she
is overcome with sadness

No idea at all

Ken Gosse generally writes whimsical, rhymed verse with traditional forms. First published in *First Literary Review–East* in November 2016, since then by Lothlorien Poetry Journal, Academy of the Heart and Mind, Pure Slush, Home Planet News Online, Spillwords, Southern Arizona Press, and others. Raised in the Chicago suburbs, now retired, he and his wife live in Mesa, Arizona, with rescue dogs and cats underfoot.

This is Ken's sixth appearance in a Southern Arizona Press anthology.

AN EVE TO REMEMBER
(a 50-word Abecedarian Poemid*)

By

Christmas
Day, the

eve before
forever
gone, except

how it's cherished
in families:
joined together,
kissing aunts and

loving grandparents;
magic in the air;
nocturnal visit
on the horizon;
presents piled high,

queued carefully,
realizing
some for children,
tots, and toddlers

urgently
vie for their
welcoming,

x-rayed,
youthful

zeal.

~~

*About the poem's form:

-- An Abecedarian is a form using the letters of the alphabet sequentially, usually for the first letter of each line.

-- A Poemid is a form created by Dan Brook in which each stanza has the same line-count and syllable-count and each stanza increments that count by one:
1 line of 1 syllable; 2 lines of 2 syllables each; 3 lines of 3 syllables each, etc.

OUR CHRISTMAS GUEST

There's a tree in our house that's been dressed with great care
(not the house, Heavens no! but the tree we brought there,
although not really we, because this year, you see,
I waited at home till a quarter past three
while my wife found the tree on her own, without me,
for the USPS was expected that day
though their tracking site said to expect a delay—
like the five days before, and since then, five days more—
since they'd need a 'John Hancock' on reaching our door,
then at twenty past three came my part of the chore:
to bring in the tree that I mentioned before.)

Now where was I? Ah yes! The tree, naked no more,
was propped up in a stand that we placed on the floor.
Well-designed for the task, it had six screws around
its circumference ensuring the tree that we found
would have all due support and not have to resort
to its own missing roots which were once the cohort
of its balance and feeding, which both were still needing
but now were supplied by good people who tried
to ensure its good health to the end of its days—
which were numbered, in deference to our holidays.

Until then, we'll provide it the very best care
though we burden its boughs with small colored lights' glare
and a great crowd of ornaments hung heavy there
as remembrance; nostalgia's soft annual stare
stays attentively watchful to guard against one
who assumes this tradition is all for his fun,
for the dog stays away but the cat loves to play
with the old, beat-up danglers which show signs of fray
from our past Christmas cats whom we never could teach
not to mangle the ornaments placed within reach.

Very soon, many presents encircle its girth
piling up on the floor, wrapped with colorful mirth,
tied with ribbons and bows (though no longer required
"because transparent tape," yet still highly desired),
with tags attached tightly or taped into place
for the cat, once again, with his delicate grace
assumes anything loose must be his for the taking
(as proof, he's aloof while it's visibly shaking
beneath a rogue paw as it plays the outlaw
which precedes the full pounce of his sharply-toothed maw).

And so, once again we prepare for a season
to celebrate life, love, and laughter, the reason
we gather together beneath these strange trees
which we cull from the woods, store, or box (without ease),
but our annual efforts' results always please
once we've finished the task, bought and piled the gifts,
get together with family, when focus shifts
from a dinner-time feast on a table well-set
and we circle around in the warmth we have found
in a raucous enjoyment where joy will abound
as we share our delight in a welcome well-met.

Originally published online on December 25, 2020, by Sparks of Calliope, https://sparksofcalliope.com/2021/12/25/two-poems-by-ken-gosse/

Joan McNerney has been the recipient of three scholarships. She has recited her work at the National Arts Club, New York City, State University of New York, Oneonta, McNay Art Institute, San Antonio and the University of Houston, Texas, Published worldwide in over thirty-five countries, her work has appeared in literary publications too numerous to mention. Four Best of the Net nominations have been awarded to her. *The Muse in Miniature, Love Poems for Michael* and *At Work* are available on Amazon.com A new release entitled *Light & Shadow* explores the recent historic COVID pandemic

12 STEPS TO WINTER

1. Kicking up piles of foliage,
the wind tries to enter my house.

2. I can see my breath right
in front of me now.

3. Maple leaves, oak leaves, all fall
leaves tumbling through air.

4. Window panes clattering like
nervous teeth at midnight.

5. Frost pinches my cheeks, kissing me.
A cool, cruel lover.

6. Quickly, quietly needles of snow
embroider tall fir trees.

7. That must be my friends stamping
their boots outside.

8. As the kettle boils, aromas of hot
cider spice the kitchen.

9. Our favorite Christmas songs
stream through hallways.

10. Sparkling butter cookies melting
in our mouths.

11. A tiger cat with big green eyes
tosses balls of yarn.

12. Galaxies of snow stars whirling
every which way.

Ray Whitaker has been writing both prose and poetry since he was seventeen. He has three books published from Newness Twoness Books: *ACKNOWLEDGMENT: Poems From The 'Nam*, a two-volume set [2019, 2nd Editions available on Amazon]; and *23, 18*, [2020, 2nd Edition, available on Amazon, and *For The Lost and Loved*. [2021, available on Amazon]. A chapbook, *THE SCUPPERNONG WORKS* was published last fall, also by Newness Twoness. His fifth poetry book is now at publishers for consideration, *THE TAVERN ON OLD LOG CABIN ROAD*. Ray has done readings around the state of North Carolina and Colorado, is a member of the North Carolina Poetry Society, and has been a member of The North Carolina Writer's Network. He has thrice been a "Writer-in-Residence" at the North Carolina Center For The Arts and Humanities, at Weymouth, in Southern Pines, North Carolina.

He is the father of two daughters, and lives in Colorado Springs, Colorado. Active in the poetry scene in Colorado, Ray is available for readings state-wide. Ray, an American poet, has participated in the International Poetry scene as well, published by literary journals in Bali, India, Belgium, Pakistan, United Kingdom, Greece, Ireland, and the United States.

THE OBOE PLAYER

The Christmas tree danced a little
with each new decoration placed to dangle on limbs,
and when the tree lights were turned on
the stereo's festive music
a mix of older and more contemporary music
the tree seemed just happy.

I heard an oboe in the instruments
playing on one of those tunes
such a nice blend of harmonious holiday sounds.
Somehow the oboe seemed a bit more in the mix.

Behind the tree on the wall
hangs an old painting in a golden, gilded frame.

When placing a red and white striped ball
hanging it on the tree near the painting, just so
I noticed again as if having never seen it before
the man playing the oboe in the frame
the fine brush strokes showed his face
his lips on the double-reed mouthpiece
a look of the pleasure musicians get when immersed
he was moving, swaying in the rhythm
of The Carol of The Bells.

When he saw me looking, in astonishment
he winked at me, and didn't miss a note.

WHEN TOYS WERE TAKEN SERIOUSLY

Part of the mystery and joy of the season
was my sister who seemed to place
the Christmas tree balls intently
even now, she looks like she did
a memory of when she was twelve
and I was almost six.

Today she is the prime mover
about the Christmas Tree decorations
the Moravian star atop, the strung lights
the festive wooden nutcrackers on the mantle
those things come always with her holiday intent
making things happy, all of us know this

and count on her
caring for that
as if
there is, or was
no one else
that could do it as well.

She is twelve again, and I am almost six
in those moments, remembering
wholly impatient for presents to open
being grateful
for who she was [keeping me from opening some]
and who
she has become.

Judge Santiago Burdon's Odyssey began in the "City of Big Shoulders," as Sandburg called it in his poem "Chicago." He was born during Mayor Richard Daley's first days in office and Eisenhower's first term as President.

His father named him Judge, hoping he would pursue a career in law. He had no idea his son would end up appearing in front of so many.

Santiago attended universities in the United States and abroad, focusing his studies on Victorian Literature and Authors. His short stories and poems have been featured in over two hundred fifty magazines, on-line literary journals, podcasts, and anthologies. He was recognized in Who's Who of Emerging Writers 2020 and again in 2021.

Santiago has had seven books published in the past three years.
Two collections of poetry; *Not Real Poetry* and *Tequila's Bad Advice Poetry With The Worm*.

Five books of short stories; *Stray Dogs and Deuces Wild Cautionary Tales*, *Quicksand Highway*, *Fingers In The Fan*, *Lords of the Afterglow Renegades and Noblemen*, and *Overdose of Destiny Impulse Fiction*.

Santiago became a Septuagenarian turning 70 last July. He plans to relocate to Austin, Texas from Costa Rica this winter.

WISHING I WAS THERE

I'm sitting here thinking about my folks
It feels like years since I've been home
I've got a feeling like I'm homesick
But it's something more
My thoughts are running wild
In this warm desert air
Wishing I was there
I hear those old dogs barking
As I walk up the road
It's sad because I never seem to find the time
To even write them a couple of lines
It's always phone calls home
For the Holidays
When I was young they found time for me
They worked so hard to raise a family
Now all the kids have grown
And they've grown old
Nothing more to show except for growing old

Somehow it doesn't seem right
My parents raised me then almost overnight
I heard the wind call my name
I was gone
Now I wonder what they get in return
For all the years of love and concern
I guess the person I've become is their only reward
Whenever I was down on my luck
My ole man he'd slip me a couple of bucks
And never made me feel like any less of a man
Now I've found it's not money or gifts they give
I've been a taker all these years I've lived
I never realized the true worth of their lives
The gift they give comes from their souls deep inside
That's something you can't buy

I've put so many miles between me and them
It's gotten so easy to pretend
There's no debt owed
I've got a life of my own
After all these years I hope it's not too late
To let them know I'm proud of my name
And a chance to thank them
For everything they've done
Now I'm haunted by memories
Of the way things used to be
I can hear them both calling me home
I wish I could go back to my younger days
I was cheated by yesterday
I was never told
I'd have to watch them grow old
I didn't know they'd get so old
When did they grow so old
Growing old

I'm sitting here thinking about my folks.

Hanna Hays is a lover of literature from Alamosa, Colorado. She holds an MFA in Creative Writing/Poetry from Western Colorado University and teaches 9th and 10th grade English Language Arts at Center High School. She is a self-proclaimed writer of "dead dad poetry," and uses writing as a way to process grief and to share her experiences with others, so that they may see themselves reflected in the work and maybe find their own solace. Her poems have recently appeared in Twenty Bellows and Duck Head Journal, with a poem published in the latter being nominated for a Pushcart Prize in 2022.

THE SQUEAKY SPOT

I am twenty-eight,
midnight, Christmas Eve,
I can't risk light
in a dark house;
Mom sleeps soft.
My hand slides along
peach paint textured
like tiny canyons,
tiptoe memorized path
through kitchen,
living room, hallway.
I pause before
the squeaky spot
outside Mom's door.

I am eight,
stealth mission
to meet my brothers
at the Christmas tree.
We can't risk light
in a dark house;
Mom sleeps soft.
Tiptoe turns squawk
on the squeaky spot.
Accusing glares
from the living room
burn through me as
we wait, listen…
exhale, escape.

I join co-conspirators
to ignite tree lights.
Caution required:
the current set
screams an 8-bit
Angels We Have
Heard on High.
Matthew gives cue,
Adam flips switch,
I tackle control box,
press button,
stifle joyous strains.
Gloria! In excelsis deo!
Gloria! In excelsis deo!

Silent tree casts
stained glass colors
across gifts, illuminates
record player,
acoustic guitar,
American Girl doll.
Grins grow:
Santa found us, after all.
Our first holiday
as children of divorce,
we didn't know
if we could have
Christmas twice,
once with Dad,
again with Mom.

I am twenty-eight,
midnight, Christmas Eve.
I step over
the squeaky spot.
Mom asleep for hours,
brothers doze in
burgundy armchairs
by Christmas tree
and still warm fireplace.
I climb into cream sheets,
my childhood bed, grateful
that in spite of whatever
was once broken,
tonight we are whole.

Kenneth Robbins is the author of seven published novels, two collections of poetry, forty published plays, numerous essays, stories, and memoirs on-line and in peer-reviewed journals, and a collection of short stories. His fiction has received the Toni Morrison Prize and the Associated Writing Programs Novel Award. His plays have been recognized by receiving the Charles Getchell Award, the Festival of Southern Theatre Award, and the Gabrielle Society Humanitarian Award. His radio plays have been aired over National Public Radio and the BBC Radio 3. He holds a PhD from Southern Illinois University and a MFA from the University of Georgia. He currently lives in Ruston, Louisiana, recently recognized as Professor Emeritus Liberal Arts, Louisiana Tech University.

GRANNIE HUGS

The joy of Christmas was done,
At least for us kids,
By nine each Christmas morning,
Replaced by Grannie visits
That took the rest of the day.
Put the toys away and
Get in the car.
That was the command.

Can I take my beebee gun,
I wanted to know,
It being the one gift left just for me
By Santa under our tree.

No, just get in the car.
We're late already.
Grannie's waiting,
And Christmas can't be Christmas
While Grannies wait.

So, off we set for town
With gifts wrapped with ribbons,
Christmas joy left at home.
Off to Grannies, both of them,
And slices of stale fruit cake,
Potato salad, ambrosia,
And watery iced tea.

Both Grannies were fussy—
Why didn't we come more often?
Why must we wait until
Christmas morning to show up late?
Couldn't we be happier?
Couldn't we stay longer?
You shouldn't have!—

(This about the gifts we brought.)
Both Grannies the same,
Both widowed,
Both living alone, living apart,
Living miles away,
Living for days like this
And only this:
Kids to kiss, fondle, and find fault.

The hug each gave me
Was firm and warm.
Though different, both the same,
Christmas or not,
Whenever we visited Grannies.
The gifts I received, one from each,
Given long ago,
Are forgotten now.
But not the hugs.
Not those precious hugs.

One Grannie was a pillow,
Her hug like getting wrapped
Inside a cocoon of softness
And apt to smother if held too long.
She smelled of cinnamon, flour,
And cooking oil.

The other Grannie was a stick,
Her hug brittle like hard candy
And apt to shatter if held too tight.
She smelled of snuff and cotton
And lingering cigarette smoke.

Both precious, especially on
Christmas morning, especially then,
Even now, though both are gone.
All other gifts are forgotten,
But not the hugs.
Not those precious hugs.

Shirsak Ghosh is a State Aided College Teacher at Serampore Girls' College, West Bengal, India. He is a faculty member of this college for a few years. Besides teaching, which is his profession, he composes some creative poems. He has composed some poems published in following journals like *IJELLH*, *Literary Herald*, *Literary Cognizance,* and *GNOSIS*. Some of his poems were published in different edited books like *Aulos: An Anthology of English Poetry*, *Insulatus: An Anthology of Modern English Poetry*, *Otherwise Engaged: A Literature and Arts Journal*, *Contemporary Visions: An Anthology of Poems*, *Love Letters in Poetic Verse*, *A Caged Heart*, *Dream World*, *The Beauty of Friendship*, *Love is a Divine Fragrance*, and *COVID-19: Impressions on Society*. He also published his poem in Indian Periodical.

HOME FOR THE HOLIDAYS

It's home for the holidays, my dear ones;
Christmas carols and cakes have been waiting for so long,
Jesus calls by the gift of grace and wisdom.
Time for you and us and of course our lovely X-mas tree.
Jingle Bells all around the floor arousing God's blessing
For you, me and us. Isn't it a moment of tranquil bliss
Spreading from the Heaven's kingdom?
A moment of togetherness with my loved ones.
Winter, you're the epitome of exceeding holidays
An element of euphoria and cloud nine for me.
Reading Eliot's Waste Land makes me far closer to you.
Holidays for every part of the corner of the world
Making life serene and beautiful for us.
Most importantly beckons me of Santa's call.

Colin James has a couple of chapbooks of poetry published. *Dreams of the Really Annoying* from Writing Knights Press and *A Thoroughness Not Deprived of Absurdity* from Piski's Porch Press and a book of poems, *Resisting Probability* from Sagging Meniscus Press.

TEN-THOUSAND SCHIZOPHRENIC SHAKESPEARES

Any self-taught musician can sit
listening, contentedly recording.
It's the one lone hapless tape
that insufferably defies me
answering back when I can't be bothered.
Song lists attached to burlesque breasts,
music spluttering slang,
I have a feeling for this.
Your mother asked me to find you.
She was dressed in that old housecoat,
coughing up huge gobs of guilt.
It was pointless to argue.
The new fallen snow impeded me not
since a booth at the nearest bar
was occupied by yourself.
I saw that you were unhealthy,
had the dimmest of prospects.
You offered to buy me a drink
but the look in your eyes said
you had given up perhaps as far back
as the eighth grade when Miss Clark
asked you to name the largest continent
and you said, "Australia!"

Dibyasree Nandy began writing during the lockdown period of the Covid-19 situation. Since then, she has authored The Labyrinth of Silent Voices-Epistles from the Mahabharata, Stardust-Haiku and Other Poems, Fireflies Beneath the Misty Moon, Meteor Shower, April Verses, The Terrorist's Journal and An Upset Inkpot. Her works have appeared in 70 anthologies and literary journals, both prose and poetry. She holds two Master degrees in science and technology.

BACK TO THE FISHING VILLAGE

Midst squalor and grime and lingering snow grey
It oars to a stop, my little boat
From the town of mists and smoke
Back to this hamlet where naught but fish are caught.

The creaking of old wood and putrid barrels on their side-
A room of grease with a lamp and linen torn-
Ice-layered roofs and swirling flakes at eve-
Back I have stepped into this forsaken bourg
Where I once lived
In poverty, stooped.

The cracked lantern beneath the eaves
With reckless abandon, swung
The wild wind raced past the planks
Rattling sounds boded ill and cold.

I walked towards the folk huddled around the flames
A wan glow spreading
They greeted, they waved, they welcomed me into the fold.

A hook plunged into the rimy stream
And filthy tin plates filled
Burnt fish that turned to ashes in my mouth
And yet, this was home.

A DRUNKEN HOLIDAY

The cart rolled up the cobbled street
Me, languid at the back
In the Yuletide spirit, a generous lift
As memories crumbled
Like autumn's last maple, brittle and cold.

Old Jimmy limped a bit more
Happily, Kenny skipped about, grown
Martha's pretty hair had turned long
The rustic scents had not changed
Green speckled with snow.

By the fence, a phantom of my sister standing
Waiting to greet
A ghost of a smile was thrust through my breast
Sharp as my late aunt's kitchen knife, fork.

The fireplace was dead
The armchair mildewed
Portraits needed dusting
Their subjects concealed behind ashen ages that unfold.

Lost behind Time's thick shroud
Grandma's Christmas cake
And streamers draped over Grandpa's wizened arms
No luncheon laid out upon the table musty
No firs and holly and presents stacked.

I tossed my suitcase upon the rickety bed
Brought out the one sandwich I had roughly packed
Unevenly sliced, just cucumbers thrown in
No eggs, no cheese, 'twas as dry as parchment yellowed.

Akin to a rabid beast, the room
Threatened to sink its fangs into my hollowed chest ...
Out I dashed
Towards the rowdy local pub
Where I could drink myself to death.

Joan Leotta plays with words on page and stage. She performs tales of food, family, strong women. Internationally published as an essayist, poet, short story writer, and novelist, she's a two-time Pushcart nominee, a Best of the Net nominee, and a 2022 runner-up in Robert Frost Competition. Her essays, poems, creative non-fiction, and fiction appear in Impspired, Ekphrastic Review, Verse Visual, Verse Virtual, Gargoyle, Silver Birch, Yellow Mama, Mystery Tribune, Ovunquesiamo, Synkroniciti, MacQueen's Quinterly, SoFLoPoJo, and many others in US, UK, Australia, Germany, and more. Her poetry chapbooks are *Languid Lusciousness with Lemon*, and *Feathers on Stone*, published by Main Street Rag.

A LETTER TO THE NEW OWNER OF OUR ROUND OAK TABLE

Dear Friend,

For twenty years we talked with each other
and with so many guests, of Ninja turtles,
the real Donatello and Michelangelo,
detritus and achievements of daily life.
The nicks on its surface are from where
we played cards, built gingerbread houses,
devoured favorite meals,
birthday cake, read the paper—
that solid oak surface lending gravitas
to even our most frivolous activities.
Holiday meals meant covering the oak
with gaily decorated linens,
covering it with carefully saved
fancy dishes filled with
recipes from our grandmothers, things
we ate at every holiday.
And when the festivities were over,
Dishes washed, linens in the laundry,
I would often sit sipping coffee,
gazing out our kitchen window, daydreaming,
King Arthur had his round table.
This was the round table of our kingdom.
May it serve you equally well,
as your kingdom's platform
to serve up love and joy.
Merry Christmas.
Happy New Year.

Warmly,
Oak Table's former family

CHRISTMAS LETTERS

Close to midnight on
Christmas Eve,
when everyone else has gone to bed
I fill stockings.
Oranges, chocolates, pens, and little silly gifts.

One stocking, for these past few years,
has remained bereft of goods
until I decided to fill it with words.
Some write letters to all the world,
highlighting year's events.
My pen recounts instead, how much
We missed you, beloved son,
at all the year's celebrations
all gone by without your
witty remarks, comforting hugs.

Eighteen letters, folded missives of
missing you fill the stocking now.
Each written on that evening when
when the pain of loss seems so
sharply etched upon
my heart that I can hardly breathe.
Each recounts moments of another year
passed without your presence.

Only words.
And tears.

John Wojtowicz grew up working on his family's azalea and rhododendron nursery and still lives in the backwoods of what Ginsberg dubbed "nowhere Zen New Jersey." Currently, he teaches social work at Stockton University. He serves as the Local Lyrics contributor for the Mad Poet Society blog and has been featured on Rowan University's Writer's Roundtable on 89.7 WGLS-FM. Recent or forthcoming publications include: *Rattle, Split Rock Review, Soundings East, West Trade Review, Ekphrastic Review,* and the *South Florida Poetry Journal.* He is the author of the chapbook, *Roadside Attractions: a Poetic Guide to American Oddities.*

Find out more at: www.johnwojtowicz.com

O CHRISTMAS TREE

Cotton-ball-bearded
Santas. Bucktooth school pictures
in puzzle piece frames.

Clothespin reindeer
with pipe cleaner antlers
and pom-pom
red noses.

Popsicle stick
snow men. Pony bead
candy canes. Cross-stitched
stars. Button wreaths.

Pinecone gnomes
with felt hats. Glitter-dusted
gingerbread men.

You and I kissing, tangled
on the skirt like bare
and sequin-less roots;

a googly-eye among
the pine needles in your hair
that we set aside
to hot glue back on tomorrow.

Matt McGee writes in the Los Angeles area. In 2023 his work has appeared in Spectrum, *Gnashing Teeth*, and *The NonBinary Review*. When not typing he drives around in rented cars and plays goalie in local hockey leagues.

STAYING HOME FOR THE HOLIDAYS

I fell off a roll-away ladder
at my corporate auto parts job
three days before Christmas, 2001.
Maybe it was the tangled earbud wires
piping in Jack Benny's version of 'The Man
Who Came to Dinner' circa 1949, an all-star cast
if ever one had been assembled. The studio audience
that night expected Jack to make them laugh, and laugh
they did; I was no exception, cracking up when Jack
announced he'd be suing Mr. Stanley for $150,000
after that infamous slip on an ice patch. I went
down four steps onto a tile floor, giving me
a hairline crack and a cast for the holiday,
a stroke of luck actually, since all I'd
wanted from Santa Claus that year
was a long, extended vacation.

SPIRIT OF HOLIDAYS PAST

It was a Christmas treat unto myself
the way some single people populate their
trees with gifts to themselves and their dog.
Sometimes the surprise is genuine; they found the
little thing on Amazon weeks earlier and forgot
having ever ordered it, though the dog has known
for weeks those rawhide chews have been
waiting since the 12th.

I made sure Christmas night was slow
having politely declined invitations with
elaborate stories of being busy with work,
eventually finding myself affront the local
Jack in the Box where a homeless guy slept
bundled up on the handicapped ramp. I bought
a bag of burgers, kept one and handed him the bag,
which he retrieved with cold-stiffened fingers, drawn
into his body like an electric blanket, a holiday
gift of warmth, good cheer and seasoned meat.

Back in the car I half-peeled the wrapper,
bit into the fresh food, opened the tablet and
like a surprise gift from the YouTube gods came a
compilation of 70's sitcom Christmas specials;
WKRP, MASH, Laverne & Shirley, a Three's Company
with my late cousin in a diner scene. This season had it all:
the spirit of family, of giving, and of Christmas past,
made glorious once again.

Jill Crainshaw is a professor, theologian, and poet who teaches at Wake Forest University in Winston-Salem, North Carolina. Jill and her two pups, Bella and Penny, look for poems in their backyard. Sometimes Jill writes them down.

ADVENT PRELUDE

december sun puddled on the sanctuary carpet.
splashing in the light, they swirled, twirled,
danced while people settled into empty pews.

child poet-prophets, eight years, five, only three,
they swayed, tender trees seeking, reaching,
spilling morning gold from their hands,

unrehearsed, as far as we knew, and unplanned
except perhaps by angels, if you believe in such things.
we heavy-footed grownups beheld them, wondering.

and they danced on, in the light,
in front of the remembrance table where
bread is broken, marriage vows spoken and where

on that day? innocent joy
graced wilderness-weary waiting eyes
with a wreath of swirling, spinning stars.

the music stopped, and they scampered
away down the aisle. I rubbed my eyes--
yes. their feet left a trail of stardust.

the way was prepared.

CHRISTMAS CONFECTIONS

i think it must have been peppermint
that he gave her
reaching out with
a sleight of hand
and a wisp of a smile
the day he buried his dad
cough drops are fine
butterscotch buttons too but
i think on that day
it was peppermint—
red bird peppermint puffs
to be precise
the kind that crinkles
when a piece escapes
from its cellophane wrapper
into your hand
one is enough
to savor a while
if you can keep from
biting into its sugary softness
crisp coolness tingling
your tongue with
sweet promise

Jeanine Stevens latest publications: *No Lunch Among the Day Stars* (Cold River Press, 2022), and chapbooks, *Ornate Persona* (Clare Songbirds Publishing House, 2022), *Tea in the Nun's Library* (Eyewear Publishing, UK 2022). She is winner of the MacGuffin Poet Hunt, WOMR Cape Cod Community Radio National Award, The Ekphrasis Prize, and The William Stafford Award. Jeanine has been published in *Evansville Review*, *North Dakota Review*, *Chiron Review*, *The Kerf*, *Muse and Two Thirds North* (Sweden). Jeanine studied poetry at University of California Davis, received her M.A. at California State University Sacramento and has a doctorate in Education. Instructor at American River College. Other interests include Tai Chi, collage, and Romanian folk dance.

A TRADITION

Mother serves oyster stew and little crackers
from a box with a red lighthouse. A stew—
just oysters and butter floating in warm milk.

She sings "Away in a Manger,"
the same voice as her eighth-grade solo
on the radio in Appleton.

With thick gloves, father casts spun glass
over the tree. His tune,
"It Came Upon a Midnight Clear."

We wait until the clock chimes nine,
crawl under our Hudson Bay blankets,
warm, safe, and scratchy.

In the morning, maybe a book about insects,
a board game, a blue sweater. We hope
oranges from Florida for breakfast.

Waking in the dark, ice crystals inside
our window—scent of sea and balsam,
that soft silence just before snow starts to fall.

Luisa Kay Reyes has had pieces featured in *The Raven Chronicles, The Windmill, The Foliate Oak, The Eastern Iowa Review,* and other literary magazines. Her essay, *Thank You,* is the winner of the April 2017 memoir contest of *The Dead Mule School of Southern Literature.* Her Christmas poem was a first place winner in the 16th Annual Stark County District Library Poetry Contest. Additionally, her essay *My Border Crossing* received a Pushcart Prize nomination from the Port Yonder Press. Two of her essays have been nominated for the Best of the Net anthology. With one of her essays recently being featured on *The Dirty Spoon* radio hour.

LET THERE BE LIGHT

In the very beginning The Good Lord said
Amidst the formless void, "Let there be light."
And the light from the darkness was shed
Pleasing Almighty God with its sight.

Although His Good Word is a light to our path
The darkness for several held some sway
Who blithely ignored the tragic aftermath
Of keeping kind virtue always at bay.

Thus it appeared that the light was forever gone
With the warmth and the glow of a candle
Being the only hint of a Heavenly echelon
Faith could keep from the stealthy vandal.

But then a single star on Christmas night
Revealed to all that The Light of the World
As it shone brightly with all of its might
Had come to show The Truth was unfurled.

For The Light of Life as a baby was born
As Christ came to help us live in the light
With His Great Light the earth to adorn
Pledging, "Let there be light", to hold upright.

Dr. Genalyn Panganian-Lualhati is a licensed teacher handling professional education courses such as The Child and Adolescent Development and the Learning Principles, The Teacher and the School Curriculum, Special and Inclusive Education, Special Topics in Education, Field Study, and Teaching Internship. Her extensive knowledge and background in educational management with specific focus on Educational Leadership and Teacher Professional Development, diverse teaching experience, and active involvement in professional development activities underscore her commitment to the field of education. She is also a research-based faculty member with approved research for funding in the same university. She has served as an internal examiner for student research and contributed to the scholarly community as peer reviewer of international journals. She has published research articles in Scopus-indexed journals, CHED accredited journals, ASEAN Citation Indexed journals, and in other international peer-reviewed journals and presented research papers in national and international research fora. Her research publications are dedicated to advancing teacher education by focusing on professional training and development, offering valuable insights to enhance the quality of teacher preparation programs. In addition to her academic interests, she authored poems that were internationally published in different anthologies.

LOVE ACROSS DISTANCES

Beneath the northern lights' enchanting glow,
A tale of family spans the distance, you know.
From Canada's embrace to the Philippine isles,
A yearning for kin, where warm sunlight smiles.

Home for the holidays, a fervent desire,
Across oceans wide, our hearts aspire.
Migrated souls, like migratory birds in flight,
Dream of reuniting, in the soft tropic night.

Through frost-kissed pines and snowy lanes,
Our prayers dance with the monsoon rains.
Oh, Philippines, with your shores so fair,
Bring our loved ones back, on the winter air.

In the glow of parols and lanterns bright,
A beacon of hope in the velvety night.
Across the Pacific, through stars that gleam,
May our family gather, like in a dream.

The scent of puto bumbong and bibingka sweet,
Echoes of laughter in a joyous heartbeat.
From the great white north to the archipelago's strand,
May the holiday magic bridge the distant land.

Home for the holidays, a wish we send,
May the tropic breezes on wings attend.
Canada to the Philippines, a love untold,
In the season's embrace, may their journey unfold.

A TRIO'S HOLIDAY HARMONY

In the hearth's warm glow, a family's delight,
A father, a mother, a daughter so bright.
Home for the holidays, their hearts entwine,
A tapestry of love, a festive design.

Father's hands cradle the yuletide fire,
A storyteller's whispers, a love entire.
Mother's laughter, a melody so sweet,
In the kitchen's embrace, where memories greet.

The daughter's eyes, aglow with wonder,
Beneath the twinkling lights, a bond to ponder.
Together they gather, a trio so dear,
In the magic of togetherness, joy appears.

Snowflakes dance outside, a winter's ballet,
A family's embrace, keeping chill at bay.
Stockings hung with care, secrets to unfold,
In this cozy haven, traditions retold.

Father's steady hands, a star atop the tree,
Mother's grace, a gift for all to see.
The daughter's joy, a carol in the air,
Harmony of love, a treasure rare.

A feast unfolds, a banquet so grand,
Shared laughter and stories, a holiday brand.
Turkey and trimmings, a festive array,
In this sacred circle, love holds sway.

Through the frosty window, a world transformed,
But within these walls, no heart is alarmed.
For in the warmth of familial embrace,
Home for the holidays is a sacred space.

Dr. Teejay D.Panganiban is an instructor for the undergraduate teacher education programs teaching major and professional courses at Batangas State University, The National Engineering University, JPLPC-Malvar. At present, he handles various designations such as the Program Chairperson for the Bachelor in Physical Education, Head of the Culture and Arts, Adviser of Melophiles Band, Adviser of Human Kinetics Society, and Head Coach for Sepaktakraw Team of the university.

His passion in sports, music, and arts was translated into research articles where he has published his works in *Scopus Indexed Journals*, CHED accredited journal and international peer-reviewed journal with sterling reputation. Also, his research papers were presented in national and international research fora and served as adviser and panel member for student research in the college.

He believes in the value of arming physical education students with practical, lifelong, and health skills, which cross over subject matter in order to develop a character for a positive personal, family, and community life.

A SEASON OF LOVE: OUR HOLIDAY TRIO

In the heart of winter's gentle grace,
We find our home, our sacred space,
A gathering sweet, a love so pure,
Our trio complete, our love's allure.

Autumn leaves in vibrant array,
Welcome us in a warm display.
With our baby boy, a gift so dear,
Our hearts are full, we have no fear.

His laughter, a melody, so sweet,
In our arms, his tiny heartbeat.
With every gaze and tender touch,
Our world is blessed, our hearts clutch.

The fireplace casts its golden glow,
As we watch the falling snow,
With you, my love, and our baby so small,
Our home for the holidays, we're enthralled.

In the kitchen, scents of delights,
Filling our home, these cozy nights.
Cinnamon, nutmeg, a holiday cheer,
These moments we hold, so precious and dear.

Twinkling lights and ornaments aglow,
In our home, love's enchanting flow.
As we celebrate this special time,
Our family bond, so strong, so prime.

With gratitude, we raise a toast,
To the love we cherish the most.
Our baby boy, and you, my wife,
Home for the holidays, a blessed life.

So, here's to the season, to love, to joy,
To our little boy, our precious boy.
In the warmth of our home, our hearts unite,
This holiday season, everything's just right.

Laurice E. Tolentino is an Instructor at Batangas State University TNEU JPLPC-Malvar, Philippines, where she teaches Professional and General Education courses for programs in the College of Teacher Education as well as Major subjects for programs in International Hospitality Management. Over the past two years, she has served as the College of Teacher Education's research coordinator and has also been in-charge of Food Services at the same university. She is currently acting as the department's coordinator for the Sustainable Development Goals (SDG) and the Bachelor of Technology and Livelihood Education (BTLEd). She has served as the Faculty Advisor for the Junior Hotelier and Restaurateur Association's (JHRA) from 2008-2010, 2016-2018, and 2020-2022. From 2016 to 2020, she worked as an OJT Coordinator for IHM Students.

Apart from her professional life, she has a strong interest in advancement and self-development. She always seeks fresh challenges and opportunities to acquire new skills, which highlights her value for learning new things and improving oneself.

LEAVES OF LOVE: A SINGLE MOM'S FALL JOURNEY

In the amber hues of autumn's embrace,
A single mom stands with unwavering grace.
 Leaves of gold, like whispers, gently sway,
Telling tales of strength in the fall holiday.

With a heart that beats in resilient rhyme,
She navigates the season, one leaf at a time.
A single tree, yet firmly she stands,
In the tapestry of fall, where courage expands.

Amidst the pumpkin patches and harvest air,
She weaves love and warmth with meticulous care.
A single mom, a hero in her own right,
Guiding her child through the autumnal light.

As the nights grow longer, and the air turns cool,
She kindles hope, a flame that won't be cruel.
Through the maze of challenges, she'll trail,
In the fall holiday, where strength prevails.

Under the fading light of a jack-o'-lantern's smile
She finds joy in the moments, both big and thin.
A single mom's love, a constant, steady stream,
In the fall's tender beauty, she finds her dream.

Beneath the rustling leaves, she walks with pride,
In the autumnal symphony, where dreams coincide.
With a heart full of love, and a spirit unbowed,
A single mom thrives in the fall's golden shroud

WINTER'S EMBRACE: A MOTHER-SON DREAM

In a warm corner, embraced by the fire,
A mother and son envision a cozy winter getaway.
Snowflakes dance outside, in a waltz so divine,
As they envision a getaway, a magical design.

Shining in the flickering light of the fireplace,
They plan a vacation, both merry and bright.
A pristine area covered in snow, where joy abounds,
At the bottom of the stars, in the peaceful night.

Hand in hand they stroll through the dream.
A charming plan, a winter wonderland.
White-capped mountains, a symbol of purity,
Where their hearts and souls find solace, it seems.

Sleigh riding on brilliantly snowy fields
Their spirits soar in the crisp, cold air.
The son was sparkling and light like a snowflake.
The love of his mother, a guiding, loving light.

A holiday vacation, a culinary feast,
Where hearts believe and memories are created.
In the enchanted moments when love connects,
An intricate web of unity, as winter imagines.

When night falls and the fire crackles,
Son and mother treasure the dream greatly.
When winter is peaceful and the air is clear,
They cherish the love that binds, without fear.

Paul Brucker, a marketing communications writer, lives in Mt. Prospect, Illinois, "Where "Friendliness is a Way of Life." He put a lid on poetry writing when he went to the Northwestern University grad ad school in a questionable attempt to learn how to think like a businessman and secure a decent income. Nevertheless, he has succumbed to writing poetry again.

He has been published recently in *The Literary Nest, Tokyo Poetry Journal, The Decadent Review, Pennsylvania Literary Journal, Prachya Review, The Bangalore Review, Months to Years* and *The Pagan's Muse: Words of Ritual, Invocation and Inspiration.*

AN EDIBLE LUNCHEON

The novice butler, quiet and dull as air itself,
precedes each guest within a breath of mother,
announces the arrival's name, then stands aside.
Our centerpiece -- linen, needlework and lace -- matches our
    placements.
No one, I think, notices that it's 22 inches, not the proper 30.
No one laments Miss Otis, charitable sewing queen, who sent
    regrets
for attorneys Ogle and Worm filled her void.

Mother displays her famous gold and jet bracelets
on freckled, stout, dry arms.
Hatless, she looks unexpectantly cheerful in the fresh sun.

Hours of pleasant conversation ensue:
Another minor business associate summoned to jail,
the shocking truth about gasoline mileage,
the best tobacco to utilize
when fishing, supervising the garden or whatever.
And various accounts of the 25 new acts,
which include Tyrone the Terrible,
Ollie, an Anti-anxiety Albino,
and the Giant Squeaky Wheel of Death.

The time comes to shower Alice Toplofty Gilding with lovely
    gifts.
But, her lips and jaw reveal no taste or judgment.
In fact, her veiled face and gloved hands
imply that ugliness or dilapidation lurk behind.

With vast effort, father shoulders his business cares aside
to respond to all remarks
with silly smiles and brief, dry nods.
Finally, at 2 o'clock, an edible luncheon is served.

Elizabeth Smit-Smit (with no qualifications
to the better class except a bank account
and a skin two sizes two small)
misholds an asparagus stalk,
letting its juice run down her arm.
This fatally affects the opinions of all.
Mr. Worm, for instance, clears his throat several times
    unnecessarily,
Charles, flush-faced, flares his nostrils
and mother's eyes bulge with aghast.

Then, the Senator, forever dignified and reserved,
attacks his corncob with as little ferocity as possible.
Though a tempest of choking follows, he remains agreeable,
employing a gallant gulp, aware that food, however loathsome,
once taken in mouth
must be swallowed unless it contains bones or stones.

Fortunately, sister also successfully swallows -- her feelings.
That's how she appears good, useful and lovely
despite wearing opal, the essence of bad luck.
Last night, she "rested unhappy on her bed,
flooded with the fancies of her fevered head."
The reason? The oaf
who effusively laughs over her least remark,
pout or the shake of her flyaway curls.
(Once, in the boathouse, his hand on her bosom
allegedly stirred her soul's desire and delight.)
This "man" annoys us with attentions that lead nowhere.
His social position and standard entirely differ from ours,
and he lacks the faintest idea of what constitutes a gentleman.
Doesn't sister realize that an engagement is doomed
if a father refuses?)

Well, her complaints, sighs and snarls
cannot last forever.
She begins college next year,
(probably to major in idle chatter)
and they'll be oafs galore to take his place.

Grandfather endures the lamb
growing cold on his plate.
Butler indiscreetly brings medicine on a tray.
But science can't stop pink mice
that nibble within the catacombs
of the old man's eyes.

For distraction's sake, mother suggests we all
get a jump on autumn with a new hat
and visit Woodies before our sizes are gone.

Next, ice cream is served
and the daughters of Senator and Mrs. Wheeler
dance adequately to "Sweet Adeline" and "Tarara-boom-de-day."

After meal's end, people, lacking tact and social grace,
just sit on and on through the long scattered light.
A full half hour passes unprofitably
until brother, in captivating new straw hat, starts pacing.

(I'll let you in on a secret:
Brother's not the care-free social wit and flirt
others fancy him to be.)
He dabbles in unmentionable horrors,
unappreciative that baseless fear kills
more people than legitimate danger.

Finally, brother begins to walk
and, going forth, a rabbit crosses the way --
a sure sign of misfortune.
Perhaps, only I see brother's constant companion -- sorrow.
(He disparages this best friend because it's not the genuine article,
not deep or ennobling enough.)
Nevertheless, sorrow follows,
trailed by sundry harpies, furies, ghouls and gods.
I know the route brother will take:
Larkin Lane, past city hall
and the miserable new mechanics' pavilion
(where they proudly offer free rest rooms
but charge a modest fee for the rest of the museum).
He'll end up among the grass at St. Brigid's
to lie beside our plot
and listen to the bells
as if it's extraordinary that one must die.

Meanwhile, leaves from next door blow across our lawn
and distant dogs bark their unfathomable purpose.
The Senator and kin make farewells,
cueing others to slowly depart.

Father seizes the moment for a brisk and masterly decision.
Believing it's every gentleman's duty to bequeath the wealth
of intellect as well as wallet to his children,
he issues us a special charter:
"You are the builder of your own fortune.
And minds are stronger than fortune.
Therefore, no one can hurt you except yourself."

As I watch Ms. Smit-Smit's spoiled hand wave bye-bye
and the last drop of lime dissolves on my tongue,
I decide (daydreams and tunnel vision withstanding)
to forever feast on this day,
no matter how trivial or significant my life might become.
I shall treasure this luncheon and, by doing so,
defy the Grand Chariot of Life
that rolls on, unaffected by each pebble crushed along the way.

Anna Eklund-Cheong is a haiku poet with over 100 poems published in such journals as *Frogpond, Modern Haiku, The Heron's Nest, Acorn, Mayfly, Presence, Hedgerow, Under the Basho, cattails,* and *tinywords.* A graduate of the University of Minnesota, she has worked in customer service, marketing, editing, and library research. She divides her time between her homes in a village near Paris, France, and in Maryland, USA. As an American expat, she volunteers with several Anglophone clubs in the Paris area, teaches haiku classes for adults and children, and travels with her family. Follow her at @parishaiku on Instagram, or at Paris Haiku on Facebook. She also occasionally posts on her Paris Haiku blog website, too, at parishaiku.com

arrivals gate
all faces the same
until yours

(originally published in *Acorn: a Journal of Contemporary Haiku*, #35, Fall 2015)

****

mist on the river . . .
the Christmas Day stroll
before their return flights

(Originally published in *Blithe Spirit: Journal of the British Haiku Society*, vol. 32.1, Feb. 2022)

****

another holiday--
family at the table
and family . . . not

(Originally published in *Failed Haiku--a Journal of English Senryu*, vol. 6.64, 2021)

Dr. Catherine Phillips obtained a Ph.D. in French literature and Women's Studies from the University of Toronto (2004) and teaches principally French as a second or further language at the University of Toronto's Mississauga campus. She co-authored an intermediate-advanced French textbook (*Mise au point* 8th edition, 2018), contributed studies of the works of Hélène Cixous to colloquium proceedings and monographs such as *Cixous after / depuis 2000* (2017), and has spoken about French literature and about university language didactics at numerous conferences since 1994. She has written poetry, music, and fiction from an early age, winning Yamaha young composer awards in 1977 and 1978, reported on music, film, and invited talks for university newspapers such as the *Manitoban* in the late 80s, and contributed poetry, experimental short fiction, cartoons, commentary, and music coverage to 80s and 90s Canadian zines such as *Friction, Hip Teen, Mad Cow, the Moss Side,* and *Siren,* herself helming *The Wrath of Grapes.* She currently resides in Toronto and performs original music under the name Unheimlich Manœuvre. Her academic and creative preoccupations include the development of disciplinary competence in a second or further language, child abuse and intergenerational trauma, otherness, and intersections between music and literature.

Catherine can be contacted at:
cd.phillips@utoronto.ca
https://www.facebook.com/profile.php?id=100092663838170

COMING OVER AND STAYING HOME

it was finally her turn
to host the dinner
after endless pleading
with her own mother
the best cook in the neighborhood
who hadn't taught her to cook
Christmas at Baba and Gigi's
and again Orthodox
New Year's at Baba and Gigi's
and again Orthodox
Easter at Baba and Gigi's
I don't remember an Orthodox Easter
year after year after year after year
finally Thanksgiving dinner at our house
waiting and waiting for them to arrive
I am fourteen I am pleased and excited
why are they late they live a block and a half away
I have cards for all of us to read from
that end with each person saying
something we are thankful for
my grandmother trails off
and sits mysterious
my grandfather struggles to read
and stubborns out of
performing in this charade
picking at his plate
irritated until he erupts in Ukrainian
a language I don't understand
my dad and I are told afterwards
what he said
"why so much food
I ate like a pig before we left"
they came to our house
but stayed home for the holiday

Sa' ada Isa Yahaya is a fifteen-year-old Nigerian teenage author, poet, and a short story writer. She hails from Okene Local Government Area of Kogi State. She is a proud member of the Hilltop Creative Arts Foundation and a student of Jewel Model Secondary School Kubwa, Abuja.

She is a second runner up for the AS ABUGI National Prize For Short Story and for the 2023 National Creative Writing Competition for Secondary Schools (Poetry Category) organized by the National Copyright Commission . Her poem *Nothing beautiful lasts forever* came second in the Creators Of Justice Literary Award (Youth Category) and she was shortlisted for the 2nd Teen African Writers Awards (Prose Category).

Her works have appeared in or are forthcoming in *Kalahari Review, New Voices Magazine, Eboquills, Under the Madness Magazine, World Voices Magazine, Blue Marble Review, Stripes Lit Magazine,* and elsewhere.

THAT EVERY HOLIDAY IS THE
THRESHOLD OF BEAUTY

Tonight,
my breath is beginning
to smell like home again.
My body -
a synonym for light
and I may just morph
into a feather.
At the dining table,
beautiful souls
exhibit white incisors
and the ambiance
is choked with serenity.
Come, have a taste;
Of what home feels like.
Learn how to walk into bliss.
To love and be loved too.
It is time
for the season
of warmth / love.

Madeline Male writes in a variety of poetic forms, from rhyme and free verse to haiku and limerick. Her works have been recognized in writing contests, as well as online and print publications, including *Tiny Seed Literary Journal,* Poetry Soup's Anthology *Reflections on the Important Things,* and the Kansas Authors Club zine, *Writing from the Center.* Madeline also enjoys reading, dancing, and creating artistic photographs for magazines and websites. Much of the inspiration for Madeline's work comes from observing the natural world.

THE HOUSE ON THE HILL

This sight that brought warmth to the traveler's heart
has renewed him enough to push on and start
toward that house on the hill, as his whole body feels
reminiscent of family Christmastime meals.

That house on the hill has a great fire roaring;
the smoke drifts as high as the owl that's soaring.
Beneath the full moon, it's a wonderful night —
for that house on the hill, though, not everything's right.

Yes, the door bears a wreath and the wreath bears a bow,
as shiny and gold as a sun-setting glow.
The horse in the paddock continues her nickering,
while that fire continues her evermore flickering.

Inside, they are gathered to sing an old song,
but on the first note, they're reminded what's wrong.
Each of them silently thinks of the one who's not here.
And meanwhile, the traveller's eye drips a jovial tear . . .

He's relieved that his journey has finally ended;
time apart from his family now will be mended.
The second their eyes meet each face breaks into an exuberant
    grin;
they all laugh with delight and surprise, and hug him again and
    again.

His family's always the number one reason
he works hard to get home for each Christmas season.
And now he looks forward to hanging the garlands and helping
    to bake —
but more so, the memories they have yet to make.

FALL HAIKU

Trees lose all their leaves
The breeze loses all her warmth
Harvest brings so much

Previous anthologies from Southern Arizona Press

The Stars and Moon in the Evening Sky is a collection of 120 poetic works crafted by 65 poets from across the globe inspired by the universe around us.

Dragonflies and Fairies is a collection of 72 poetic works crafted by 34 poets from across the globe celebrating the magical and mystical creatures of folklore.

Ghostly Ghouls and Haunted Happenings is a collection of 129 poetic works crafted by 46 poets from across the globe inspired by ghosts, ghouls, and things that go bump in the night.

The Poppy: A Symbol of Remembrance examines the history of the poppy as a flower of remembrance, over 80 poems and lyrics written by World War One poets between 1912 and 1925, and 79 poems written by 21st Century poets from around the globe in remembrance of the fallen heroes from all war of the last century.

The Wonders of Winter is a collection of 120 poetic works crafted by 50 poets from across the globe that celebrate the winter season.

Love Letters in Poetic Verse is a collection of 143 poetic works written and contributed by 58 poets from across the globe celebrating romance and love.

Castles and Courtyards is a collection of 79 poetic works written and contributed by 37 poets from across the globe celebrating the medieval life of Kings, Queens, peasants, and troubadours.

Poetry Inspired by "A Midsummer Night's Dream" is a collection of 102 poems penned by 43 bards from across the globe inspired by William Shakespeare's romantic comedy *A Midsummer Night's Dream.*

Beyond the Sand and Sea is a collection of 148 poems from 48 poets from across the globe about the sea, seashore, lighthouses, or anything associated with life on or near the sea.

A Children's Book of Bedtime Verse is a collection of 95 poetic works by 34 poets from across the globe written to be read to children before bed.

Upcoming anthologies from Southern Arizona Press

Anthologies for 2024

Riding the Rails – Poems about trains and the railroad. Coming in early February 2024.

Hidden Meanings – Poems written in the Acrostic style. Coming in early April 2024.

School's Out – Poems about school and the fun of summer vacations. Coming in early June 2024.

A Day at the Park – Poems inspired by a day at a park, amusement park, water park, fair, carnival, camping, or any type of family outing. Coming in early August 2024.

Ghostly Ghouls and Haunted Happenings Vol 2 – Poems about ghosts, ghouls, haunted houses, vampires, or any of the creatures that go bump in the night. Coming in early October 2024.

Tropical Vacations – Poems about tropical or romantic vacations. Coming in early December 2024.

Poets interested in submitting works for upcoming anthologies are asked to check out our Current Submissions page at: http://www.southernarizonapress.com/current-submissions/ for more information about each anthology and our process for submission.

New independent releases from Southern Arizona Press

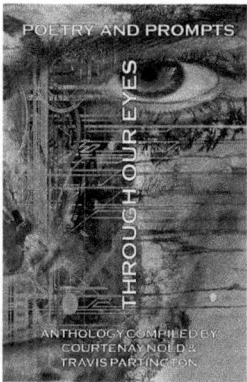

Through Our Eyes compiled by Courtenay Nold and Travis Partington. This book is unique in the way each section is based upon a prompt and offers the reader an interactive space to reflect on their own experiences with the prompt. *Through our Eyes* provides a platform for poets to write about difficult topics like trauma and PTSD. Topics we often hold as secrets behind pursued lips. We want to speak, but. This book also passively encourages readers to speak their own experiences. *Through Our Eyes* is more than a book you read, it is a book you have a conversation with.

https://www.amazon.com/dp/1960038435

I See God by Cindy Smith. One day I lost a small prop of the word *hope* at the beach. I looked on the beach at dawn the next day at dawn and did not find it. I wondered, "Did people see *hope*? Did they pick it up but not think it was theirs? Were they to focused on the clouds to notice it?" Later that afternoon, I was glad to find *hope* exactly where I had left it. If you need *hope*, it's yours for the taking. Open your heart to Jesus Christ. He is "the *hope* of the world." May you find peace and *hope* in the pages of this book.

https://www.amazon.com/dp/1960038443

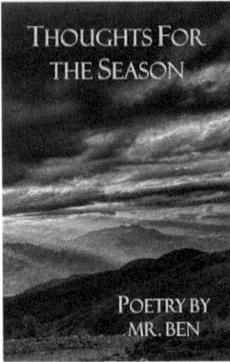

Thought for the Season by Mr. Ben. *Thoughts For The Season* is a collection of poems reflecting the emotions of people in several life situations, including the yuletide. It pens the yearnings and reactions of people in regards to matters of family, nature, love, and holiday. A book written to inspire, educate, and entertain.

https://www.amazon.com/dp/1960038451

Time Well Spent by Bill Cushing. Mr. Cushing explores the entire spectrum of his journey through life. From bullies to the horrors of military school to his first teenage crush, you will find an adventure around the next corner of this wonderful piece of literature. Thoroughly entertaining, you are sure to be entertained with this yet another creative exploration of the human condition.

https://www.amazon.com/dp/196003846X

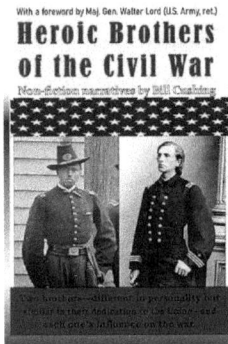

Heroic Brothers of the Civil War by Bill Cushing. *Heroic Brothers of the Civil War* focuses on two brothers' exploits fighting for the Union. "The Last Man" relates Lt. Alonzo Cushing's death during Gettysburg; he was posthumously awarded the Medal of Honor in 2014 for his actions. "The First Seal" gives a comprehensive overview of the military life of his younger brother, William, a midshipman dismissed from Annapolis for his behavior but who was reinstated to the Navy at the war's start to become one of its most daring heroes.

https://www.amazon.com/dp/1960038478

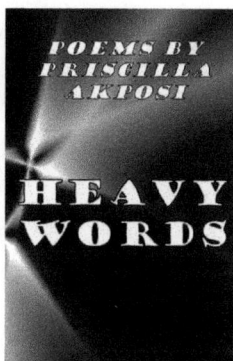

Heavy Words by Priscilla Akposi. Throughout my journey as a writer, I have come to understand the strength of balance in the human cycle. The cause - effect relationship that exists in our everyday encounter, the undeserving rewards we receive that sometimes burns our pride or fans to flame out determination. And with all these, even with all the pretense to be on the safe side with God and humanity, man falls into the coldness of the world rather than the warmth. Goodness no longer pierces the heart, one evil is enough to make man hate the world and himself. So, what if water is perpetually poured on water? It becomes rusted, the same thing when the heart succumbs to the cold of this world and forgets to keep a balance with the warmth. *Heavy Words* is penned with words that unveil the unseen warmth of the world, creating a balance to the weight of everything vile that resides in every broken heart and unites you with the peace within. I believe *Heavy Words* will be your guide to embrace that peace.

https://www.amazon.com/dp/1960038486

All titles are also available directly from Southern Arizona Press at:
https://www.southernarizonapress.com/store/

Published works by our featured contributors

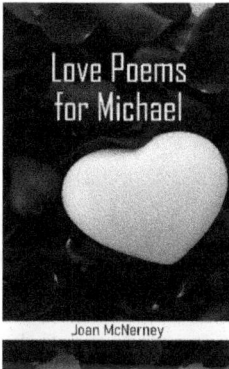

Love Poems for Michael by Joan McNerney
Many reflect on New England with autumn foliage and fierce winters. However, four seasons do include bursting springs and boiling summers. Love is its own season, its own country, its own domain. Let's explore love up north during spring and summer.

https://www.amazon.com/Love-Poems-Michael-Joan-McNerney/dp/9388319656
https://www.cyberwit.net/publications/1602

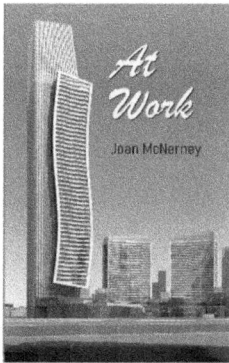

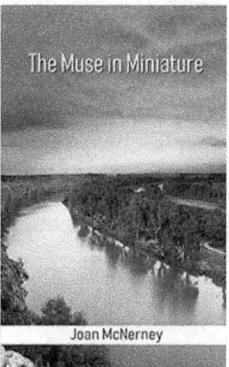

At Work by Joan McNerney explores everyday workers. It is unique because each worker, either female or male, receives their own page. These are snapshots of people who are either content with or made unhappy by their daily circumstances. Reading this book is an exploration of human nature at its core.

https://www.amazon.com/At-Work-Joan-McNerney/dp/8182537835

https://www.cyberwit.net/publications/1759

The Muse in Miniature by Joan McNerney
There is no doubt this poet very aptly traverses an immense range of emotion and experience. Here we find poetry's passion and powerful imagination in rich abundance.

https://www.amazon.com/Muse-Miniature-Joan-McNerney/dp/9389074509

https://www.cyberwit.net/publications/1262

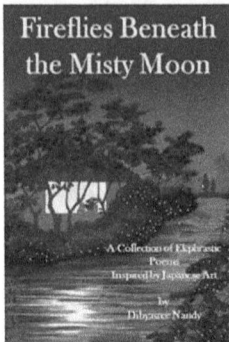

Fireflies Beneath the Misty Moon is a collection of Ekphrastic poems written by Dibyasree Nandy inspired by the works of Japanese artists Okumura Masanobu, Suzuki Harunobu, Utagawa Kunisada, Yoshitoshi Tsukioka, Kobayashi Kiyochika, Ogata Gekko, Toshikata Mizuno, Settai Komura, Torii Kotondo, and Kondo Shiun. *A Southern Arizona Press Published Book.*

https://www.amazon.com/dp/1960038125

April Verses by Dibyasree Nandy. Getting up early in the morning, savouring the clemency of the month, at the threshold of a severe summer, we turn to poetry as the means to paint a picture of the mountains and seas. *A Southern Arizona Press Published Book.*

https://www.amazon.com/dp/1960038273

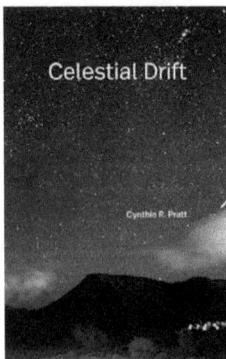

Celestial Drift by Cynthia R. Pratt. This book of poems uses the concept of constellation drift to capture how families, too, move apart. Nothing speaks to this more than having a daughter in Africa, where distance might as well be another planet, or a son needing more than a mother can give. These ties to family change but still remain spatially connected.

https://www.amazon.com/Celestial-Drift-Poetry-Cynthia-Pratt/dp/0692785701

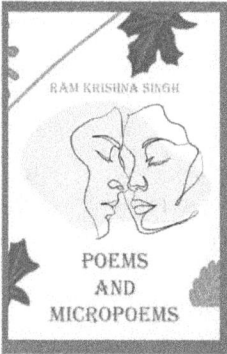

Poems and Micropoems is the newest collection of 80 haiku, 44 tanka, and 35 longer poems by Indian English poet Ram Krishna Singh, who is a creative genius of many excellences. *A Southern Arizona Press Published Book.*

https://www.amazon.com/dp/1960038087

Marianne Tefft's poetry collection is inspired by the phases of the Moon - waxing, full, waning, and new – *Full Moon Fire* traces the journey of love from bright to bittersweet and back again. Born under the Caribbean sky, these 40 "spoken songs" are romantic poems that speak to every heart that has ever loved under the full Moon.

https://www.amazon.com/Full-Moon-Fire-Spoken-Songs/dp/0228876451

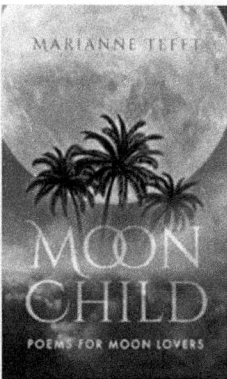

A poetry collection bathed in Caribbean moonlight, *MOONCHILD* by Marianne Tefft, celebrates winter, spring, summer, and autumn under the full Moon. With 40 romantic poems for Moon lovers, MOONCHILD speaks from the heart to all those who love in every season under the bright night sky.

https://www.amazon.com/Moonchild-Poems-Lovers-Marianne-Tefft/dp/0228882230

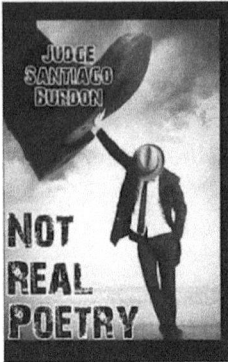

Not Real Poetry - "Judge Burdon's poetry is a sophisticated slap in the face. The imagery induces you to clear your throat and shift your weight from one side to the other. Judge doesn't waste his words in an attempt to make you comfortable. As a poet he delivers defined grit and structured devastation." - S.L. Fleurimont Editor The Remnant Leaf Online Journal October 2017

https://www.amazon.com/Not-Real-Poetry-Santiago-Burdon/dp/1914130286

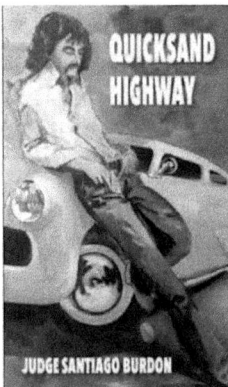

Quicksand Highway - "With tales from skid row, bars, motels and hospitals, *Quicksand Highway* tells tales of drug running, bullet dodging, drug addiction and broken romance with the insight of someone who knows what he is talking about. This collection of short stories explores life in the fast lane, extremely funny and always gritty. Judge's *Quicksand Highway* delivers the goods." - Jesse James Kennedy (Author *of Missouri Homegrown, Tijuana Mean,* and *Black Hills Reckoning.*)

https://www.amazon.com/Quicksand-Highway-Judge-Santiago-Burdon/dp/B09KNGJT6T

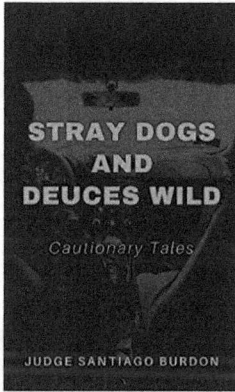

Stray Dogs and Deuces Wild – "When I first read Burdon's work I instinctively realised that here was a man who knew the score. That he was not a fake or dilettante. I could feel a bitter, hard-won experience that lay behind every line. These stories are both beautifully written and capture conclusively the humour, excitement, sadness, and disappointment of a life lived on the edge. I cannot recommend this book highly enough." - Ian Copestick   "Burdon presents a highly amusing collection of bohemian stories from the fringe. He finds literary pearls at the bottom of a dark ocean of smut and sin, propelling us into wild and unhinged terrain in a fashion similar to such luminaries as Charles Bukowski, William S. Burroughs, and Denis Johnson. Buy this book today!" —Matt Nagin

https://www.amazon.com/Stray-Dogs-Deuces-Wild-Cautionary/dp/1655287931

Tequila's Bad Advice - "Judge Santiago Burdon's poetry is a sophisticated slap in the face. The imagery induces you to clear your throat and shift your weight from one side to the other. Judge doesn't waste his words in an attempt to make you comfortable. As a poet he delivers defined grit and structured devastation. He speaks in the language of gasoline fumes and stale cigarette smoke. Always honest and fearless, never apologizing. Know that I am a fan." - S.L. Fleurimont Editor *The Remnant Leaf Journal*
A Southern Arizona Press Published Book.

https://www.amazon.com/dp/1960038168

Lords of the Afterglow - Renegades and Noblemen by Judge Santiago Burdon is a collection of sixteen bizarre, precarious, as well as comical Bohemian tales of adventurous mayhem. While working as a drug smuggler for a Mexican Cartel, Santiago; a recovering addict, ex-con, womanizer, gambler, and ill-fated pilgrim encounters situations of irresistible misfortune. Adding chaos to these events is his ex-cellmate, loose cannon, drug and alcohol fueled Colombian partner Johnny Rico. It is an expedition into twisted and hilarious states of mind and body. Every story in this collection centers on the working relationship and unique friendship of these 'Dos Chiflados' Two Whacky Guys.
A Southern Arizona Press Published Book.

https://www.amazon.com/dp/1960038249

Overdose of Destiny, Judge Santiago Burdon takes us on another wild and crazy ride. Considered to be one of the most influential writers of hard hitting and raw fiction of our time, this 21st Century "Mark Twain" has shared a book of 20 Impulse Fiction stories that a reader will find hard to put down. Each story recounts a moment in life that creates a person's character, and Santiago is certainly "a character". Whether he is addressing young teen hormones or losing one's virginity to an older woman, drug running or standing lookout for a Payphone Bandit, aiding an injured fruit bat or a Senator's ex-wife, or sharing tall tales from grizzly bears to big fish, each story will take you on an adventure with the hero winning in the end. It has been my honor to bring this book to publication.
A Southern Arizona Press Published Book.

https://www.amazon.com/dp/1960038397

My Heart is Broken: It Needs Fixing by
Catherine A. MacKenzie. There's no time limit on grief, not where the loss of one's child is concerned. Child loss is indescribable; children should never predecease their parents. After her son Matthew died unexpectedly from a rare heart cancer (after receiving an artificial heart and then a donor heart, both in under two months), she began writing a poem every month on the eleventh, the monthiversary of his death, along with other poems commemorating meaningful dates. Words describing grief and pain are limited—or are they endless?

https://www.amazon.com/dp/1927529824

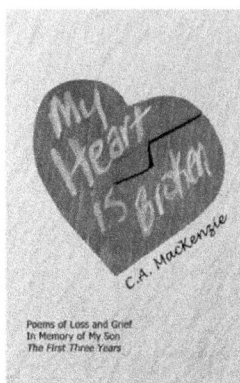

Broken Hearts Can't Always Be Fixed by
Catherine A. MacKenzie. This is the author's second book of grief poems dealing with the loss of her adult son Matthew to cancer. Written over the space of two years. Illustrated.

https://www.amazon.com/dp/1990589022

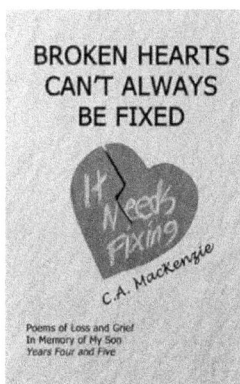

After Death Won: Poetry and Prose by
Catherine A. MacKenzie. "At the end, all we have are memories that fade away with our last breath..." A collection of poetry and prose honouring the author's late son.

https://www.amazon.com/dp/1990589170

WATCH THE BIRD FLY

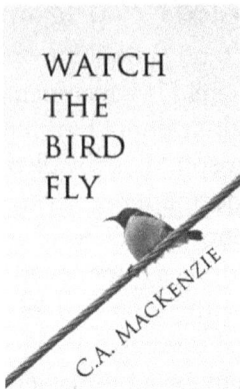

Watch the Bird Fly by Catherine A. MacKenzie. A collection of poetry.

https://www.amazon.com/dp/B0CJH7S5W7

Roadside Attractions by John Wojtowicz crisscrosses the American compass from oddities such as New Jersey's "Lucy the Elephant" to the many far-flung "Statues of Paul Bunyan." While there is humor within these pages (in "Cabazon Dinosaurs and other Stories," "Christ of the Ozarks" becomes "The Statue of Willie Nelson Wearing a Dress"), Wojtowicz is more than just a Kerouac of kitsch. His voice seduces us like a carnival barker to witness attractions like "Igloo City" and "Lady's Leg Sundial," then once we rubes are hooked, he bestows such wisdom as "Are we content to merely mourn the casualties / of our greed, ceaseless loggers / erecting monuments to commemorate clear-cut trees?" ("Grandfather Cuts Loose the Ponies"). These poems resonate with "this human urge/ to mark universal canvas" ("Cadillac Ranch"), leaving the reader to ponder the poet's question, "What more could there be to this life?" ("Near-Sighted"). What more, indeed, than these human, brilliant poems?

https://www.amazon.com/dp/1954895089

www.ingramcontent.com/pod-product-compliance
Lightning Source LLC
Chambersburg PA
CBHW060747050426
42449CB00008B/1314